FIRST PUBLISHED IN 1900

THE COMPLETE
PALMIST

NIBLO

NEWCASTLE PUBLISHING CO., INC.
NORTH HOLLYWOOD, CALIFORNIA
1982

A NEWCASTLE BOOK
FIRST PRINTING OCTOBER 1982
PRINTED IN THE UNITED STATES OF AMERICA

PREFACE.

MAN's past history and future destiny are written upon the palm of his hand!

Is this proposition to be accepted with implicit faith?

I assert that it may.

Of the Science of Palmistry, which is only a branch of Astrology, the origin may be said to date back almost to the creation of the world.

Nevertheless, let us give here a short epitome of the history of palmistry, and occupy a brief space in reviewing the principal phases through which this science has passed.

I do not consider it worth while, at this late day, to trace back history beyond the times of the Egyptians and Chaldeans, and even in regard to them there is no direct information concerning the foundation of the system to which the wise priests of Isis adhered, as also did the meditative shepherds who are mentioned in the Holy Scriptures themselves. Nor do I deem it necessary to dwell upon the period known as the Middle Ages. The struggles of the human mind to attain the knowledge of the truth were then still crude and but partially successful: they did not produce their full result until the sixteenth century, when the fine Renaissance of the intellect took place which was the beginning of the modern era.

During the Middle Ages palmistry was constantly studied and practised, but it was not until the sixteenth century that a work was published presenting a comprehensive view of the whole subject. This work was complete in its developments, ingenious and rational in its deductions; in a word, worthy to serve as the first monument to the science of palmistry as understood in those days.

During the seventeenth century the taste for the study had already become widespread; various treatises upon palmistry, written by men of eminent scientific attainments, made their appearance· one after another. Of these authors I will mention only the names of Dr. Rothman and Dr. Saunders, whose works found a place in the most famous libraries.

It was reserved for the present age to furnish palmistry with its elect apostles and a definite code—a code not based exclusively upon the mighty traditions of the past, nor upon the reflection and researches of ages gone. This code was also chiefly founded upon the discoveries of modern science and upon numberless experiments which were made again and again in the full light of publicity and frequently with the coöperation of distinguished supporters of absolute skepticism.

The first of these men took issue directly with the ancient doctrine.

Palmistry, according to Captain d'Arpentigny—for such was the name of this distinguished man—may be reduced purely and simply to cheirognomy, or merely to the study of the two hands with respect to their general shape, the form of the fingers, the form of the phalanges upon which grow the nails, and the greater or less development of the finger-joints.

D'Arpentigny's cheirognomy only presented one side of the great science of palmistry. For him the lines on the hand and their interpretation were a dead language; the close and intimate tie which unites cheirognomy with cheiromancy eluded his observation; nevertheless, to d'Arpentigny belongs the glory of having first explained the correlation between the form of the hand and man's existence. This he did, not by the help of the imperfect dissertations of the ancients, but by the intrinsic laws of this physical and animal life of which we are the centre, and of which—though, alas, only to a limited extent—we are the masters and protectors.

While we cannot insist too strongly upon the fact that Desbarrolles has enlarged the domain traversed by d'Arpentigny as well as perpetuated his doctrine, we must add that he has accepted *in extenso* the series of propositions laid down by the old soldier, Napoleon the First.

I shall follow the line of argument traced by him and his predecessors. I shall also add to the labors of those who have gone before us many personal observations, and, above all, I shall endeavor to classify all the elements to be investigated in such a manner that they may be easily and completely understood.

In a word, I intend that every reader of *The Complete Palmist* may be able, after a few hours' study, to find in it not only the information he may desire concerning himself, but also that concerning the past, the present, and the future of all those who submit their hands to his inspection.

Niblo

The Palmist

TABLE OF CONTENTS.

CHEIROMANCY.

LIST OF ILLUSTRATIONS.

Fig. 1. Spots upon a line.   Fig. 6. Chained lines.

"   2. Sister lines.   "   7. Wavy lines.

"   3. Forked terminations.   "   8. Broken lines.

"   4. Tasselled terminations.   "   9. Capillaried lines.

"   5. Ascending and descending
      branches.

Fig. 10. The Star.   Fig. 14. The Island.

" 11. The Square.   " 15. The Triangle.

" 12. The Spot.   " 16. The Cross.

" 13. The Circle.   " 17. The Grille.

Cheirognomy.

THE COMPLETE PALMIST.

SECTION I.

CHEIROGNOMY ; OR, THE SHAPES OF THE HANDS.

IT is usual to divide the science of Cheirosophy into two principal sections : Cheirognomy, or the science of interpreting the characters and instincts of men from the outward formations and aspects of their hands ; and Cheiromancy, or the science of reading the characters and instincts of men, their actions and habits, and the events of their past, present, and future lives, in the lines and formations of the *palms* of their hands. Though, as will be seen anon, the line of demarcation which has been drawn between these two branches of the science is not only false in principle but misleading in practice [for, as will be seen in the following pages, the two sections are inextricably intermingled and cannot be separated if accuracy of result is aimed at], it is still convenient to preserve the semblance of separation, so that the student may master the principle of cheirognomy before he begins to apply it to the interpretation and elucidation of the more intricate rules of cheiromancy, and for this reason the one great subject of cheirosophy has been divided into its two constituent and companion elements of cheirognomy and cheiromancy.

1.
The two branches of Cheirosophy.

Cheirognomy, therefore, is that branch of the science of the hand which enables us, by a mere superficial observation of the exterior formations and appearance of the hands, and by the impressions

2.
Cheirognomy.

produced by them on the senses of vision and of touch, to arrive at an accurate estimate of the character, disposition, and natural propensities of any individual in whose presence we may find ourselves. It is of the highest importance that the student of cheirosophy should first master this very important branch ; for what is more obvious than that the character and tendency of the mind and the natural inclinations of the subject under examination should so materially influence his actions, manner, and speech, his physical and moral bases of life, and the events of his existence—that by getting at the former by the aspect of his hands, the knowledge of the latter follows almost of itself ?

3.
Cheirognomy and Cheiromancy.

Again, it will be borne in mind that the cheirognomy of a subject—that is to say, the shape of his (or her) hands—is often hereditary and inborn, the physiological legacy of a long line of ancestors, whose characters and peculiarities of mind he may possibly inherit, whilst the lines, signs, and mounts of the palm—that is to say, the cheiromancy of a subject—are more often the results of the external and internal influences, such as the astral and cerebro-nervous fluids.

4.
The divisions of Cheirognomy.

Cheirognomically speaking, hands are divided into seven classes or types, each of which will in due course receive careful attention. Firstly, however, it is necessary to consider the interpretation of the many general features of a hand which carry with them their own significations, to whatever type that hand may belong.

SUB-SECTION I.

CONCERNING THE HAND IN GENERAL AND THE INDICATIONS AFFORDED BY THE ASPECTS AND CONDITIONS OF ITS VARIOUS PARTS IN PARTICULAR.

To whatever type a hand may belong, there are certain aspects and formations of its constituent parts which materially affect the tendencies indicated by the development of that particular type, and these aspects and conditions must be carefully considered in the preliminary examination of that hand. Such are the developments and formations of the palm, the fingers, the joints, the thumb, the relative size and proportions of the whole hand and of its constituent parts—all of which matters must be observed carefully to arrive at the true influence of the developed, or mainly developed, type ; and to explain the indications which are read in these circumstances and conditions is the aim of the present sub-section.

5.
The Seven Types.

CHAPTER I.

The Palm of the Hand.

6.
Its Indications.

IN the first place, you will notice the formation and the physiological conditions of the *palm*. In it are found the *physical* attributes of the character and the intensity with which they are developed.

7.
Thin and narrow.

If the palm is thin, skinny, and narrow, it indicates timidity, a feeble mind, narrowness and paucity of intellect, and a want of depth of character, energy, and moral force.

8.
Well-proportioned.

If, on the other hand, it is in perfect proportion with the fingers, the thumb, and the rest of the body, firm without being hard, elastic without approaching to flabbiness, the mind thereby indicated is evenly balanced, ready to accept impressions, appreciative, intelligent, and capable of sustaining and directing the promptings of

Over-developed.

the instinct. If, however, this last hand is too highly developed, and its proportions are too strongly accentuated, the exaggeration of these qualities tends to produce over-confidence, selfishness, and sensuality ; whilst if, going a step farther, the hand joins to these

Hardness.

highly developed proportions a hardness and resistance to the touch, and the palm is longer than the fingers, the character tends towards brutality of instinct, and a low grade of intelligence is betrayed by the animality of the ideas. These last characteristics are those *par excellence* of the elementary type.

9.
Hollow palm.

A hollow, deep palm denotes almost invariably misfortune, loss of money, misery, and danger of failure in enterprise. This is caused by a defection of the Plain of Mars, and is a sign of ill-luck even when the rest of the hand is favorable.

The palm, therefore, must be absolutely normal, and naturally proportioned to the rest of the hand (*i.e.*, to the thumb and fingers), and thus to the rest of the body. In any other case its indications will be found to modify these of the rest of the hand, to the consideration of which we can now turn.

10.
Necessity of normal condition.

Any excess in the formation of any part of the hand is bad, denoting disorder and demoralization of the qualities indicated by the formation which is in excess, and this is the more infallible if the phalanx of the thumb, wherein are seated the indications of *the will*, be long.

11.
Excesses of formation.

CHAPTER II.

The Joints of the Fingers.

12.
Smooth and
jointed fin-
gers.

Looking at the fingers of the whole world, they divide them-selves, cheirognomically speaking, into two great classes : (*α*) Fingers which are knotted, and (*β*) fingers which are smooth ; that is to say, (*α*) those in which the joints are so developed as to cause a perceptible "bulge" where they occur between the phalanges of the fingers, and (*β*) those in which the joints are so little pronounced as to be imper-ceptible at first sight ; and the former class divides itself again into two sub-classes : (*α* 1) those fingers which have both joints developed and (*α* 2) those which have but one.

13.
The joints.

Development of the joints of the fingers indicates thought and order, which are greater or less in their influence on the life, accord-ing as one or both joints are to a greater or less degree prominent.

14.
The upper
joint.

If the first joint [*i.e.*, that which connects the first (or nailed) phalanx and the second (or middle) phalanx] is developed, accen-tuating the junction of the first and second phalanges of the fingers, it indicates a method and reason in the ideas, a well-ordered mind, and a neat, administrative disposition. The development of this joint, if the phalanx of will [on the thumb] is long, is generally indic-ative of remarkable intelligence ; but if the phalanx of will is short, this development of the first joint often betrays excess of ill-directed reasoning, tending to paradoxicalism, and this is more certainly the case if the Line of the Head decline upon the Mount of the Moon and the fingers are pointed. When the Mount of Jupiter is high in the hand, the development of this joint denotes vanity.

If this first joint be very prominent there is always a great deal of talent in the subject; but if the lines of the palm are thin and dry, and the thumb is small, a lamentable want of soul is generally apparent. Reason, however, remains always the prevailing instinct.

If the second joint [*i.e.*, that which connects the second (or middle) phalanx and the third (or lower) phalanx] is also developed, the instincts of reason and order are the more strongly pronounced. In this case the prevailing instincts of the subject will be symmetry, order, and punctuality. The mind will be well regulated, the ideas will be good and equitable, and the actions will be governed by reflection and deliberation. There will be the love of analysis and of inquiry, and a strong *penchant* towards the sciences. Both joints thus developed, and the Mount of the Moon high in the palm, indicate a love of poetry and of music, but the poetry must be grand and reasonable, and the music will be scientific and true.

The development of the second joint only, gives to a subject order and arrangement in things material and worldly, as opposed to the orderliness in things mental and psychological, which is indicated by the development of the first [or upper] joint. The orderliness of the second joint is that which appertains to things connected with one's *self*, a selfish order which produces merchants, calculators, speculators, and egoists.

If, on the other hand, your fingers have *neither* joint highly developed [*i.e.*, no perceptible bulge is to be seen at the joints], your *penchant* will be towards the arts. Your proceedings and actions will be governed by inspiration and by impulse, by sentiment and by fancy, rather than, as in the former case, by reasoning, knowledge, and analysis, and whatever the type of the hand, if the fingers are smooth, the first impression of that subject is always the correct one, and subsequent reflection will not help him in arriving at a conclusion.

19.
Smooth
fingers with
upper joint
perceptible.

Smooth fingers with the first joint indicated by a bulge which is not very much accentuated, often denote a talent for spontaneous invention and intuition in the pursuit of science, but these qualities are never in this case the result of calculation. This first joint *rising* only on the back of the fingers, *not* bulging out at their sides, indicates a talent for invention.

20.
Bad line of
head.

When with smooth fingers the Line of the Head is bad and twisted, declining upon the Mount of the Moon, which is high, with a short phalanx of logic in the thumb, though the intuition remains, it will generally be all wrong, and give to the subject the most false conceptions.

21.
Effect of
joints.

Thus it is easily explained that whilst knotty-fingered subjects have most *taste* intellectually speaking [taste, properly so called, being born of reason and intellectual consideration], those with

Effect of
smooth
fingers.

smooth fingers have the larger share of natural and unreasoning grace. Passion [as opposed to sensuality] is the *worldly* instinct of the former, whereas sensuality [as opposed to passion] is generally a characteristic of the latter.

22.
Smooth fin-
gers.

By a like chain of argument, smooth-fingered subjects often fail in their undertakings through pursuing them too hotly and impulsively, and when with smooth fingers the Line of Head is separated from the Line of Life [477] the badness of the latter sign

Bad line of
head.

is the more pronounced, for the impulse of the smooth fingers will carry into prompt and unconsidered action the false impressions and mistaken self-confidence of the separated lines.

23.
Differences
of impulse.

Throughout the examination of hands, these two principles must be borne in mind—that the jointed subject works by calculation, reason, and knowledge, whilst the action of the smooth-fingered subject is born of and governed by spontaneity, instinct, impulse, and inspiration.

24.
Effect of
joints.

At the same time one must never lose sight of this particular ; that, though with the first joint developed a hand may betray artistic instincts, if both joints are prominent, art becomes a thing tolerated merely, and not a thing understood.

Education, self-discipline, and cultivation may develop joints in a hand, and may cause fingers originally rounded to become square, or even spatulated, but they can never erase the joints and produce a smooth-fingered hand, or mould square or spatulated fingers into roundness, for it is easier to go from artistic to scientific instincts, from intuition to knowledge, or from idealism to materialism, than *vice versâ*.

25. Development and disappearance of joints.

CHAPTER III.

The Comparative Length of the Fingers.

AGAIN, the fingers of a hand are either short or long. That is, on first sight they may strike one as being either short or long by comparison with the palm and rest of the hand, or by comparison with the majority of fingers one is in the habit of seeing.

26.
Short fingers. People with short fingers are quicker, more impulsive, and act more by intuition and on the spur of the moment, than people with long ; they prefer generalities to details, jumping hastily to conclusions, and are quick at grasping the entirety of a subject.

27.
Effect of
short fingers. They are not particular about trifles, caring little for appearances and for the conventionalities of life ; but their leading feature is their quickness of instinct and action. Their judgment is quick, and their action is prompt, and they have, to a remarkable degree, the instinct of the perception of masses. They are brief and concise in expression and in writing, but often when the rest of the hand is weak such subjects are given to frivolity and chattering.

28.
Thick and
short fingers. If the fingers are thick as well as short it is a sign of cruelty. Short fingers with a short Line of Head denote want of tact, and carelessness in acting on impulse, especially if the Mount of the Moon is

Weak hand. highly developed ; but with short nails and a long Line of Head, the instinct of synthesis [which is the great attribute of the short-fingered subject] gives a talent for grasping particulars and comprehending a scheme which produces a rare faculty for administration.

29.
Short fingers
with joints. If with short fingers either or both of the joints are developed, they will have a certain amount of reason and calculation to assist

the quickness of their intellect, which will thus be supplemented by a powerful auxiliary, for the calculation indicated by the joints will be able to apply itself with the rapidity of comprehension indicated by the shortness of the fingers.

With long fingers we find a love of detail even to frivolousness, an instinct of minutiæ which often blinds the subject to the appreciation of the harmonious whole, carefulness in dress and behavior, and consequent hate of slovenliness or brusquerie of manner. Such a subject will be respectful and dignified, easily put out, and easily pleased by an attention to the minor peculiarities of his nature.

30.
Long fingers.

If long fingers have the first joint developed, such a subject will be inquisitive, watchful, always on his guard against liberties, observant of small things, and addicted to manias and idiosyncracies about things, especially if the phalanx of logic in his thumb be long.

31.
Long fingers and upper joint.

Artists with such fingers as these will often elaborate detail at the expense of the mass of the subject upon which they are working, and all persons whose fingers present this formation will be distrustful, always trying to seek out second meanings for one's remarks, and attributing motives and deep significations to one's most meaningless speeches and most trivial actions.

32.
Long-fingered artists and others.

Long fingers, therefore, betray a worrying disposition, worrying both to themselves and to others, unless a long Line of Head and a well-developed phalanx of will modify the indications of the fingers.

33.
Effect of long fingers.

In literature such subjects pay an attention to detail which is maddening to see in print; for they go off at a tangent, and discourse on matters more or less germane to the subject in hand, until one loses sight of the prime object of the argument, which thus becomes confused and wearisome.

34.
Long fingers in literature.

Such hands, also, often betray cowardice, deceitfulness, and affectation; but these tendencies may be overruled by a good Line of Head and a well-developed Mount of Mars. [371–2.]

35.
Bad effects of long fingers.

36.
Long fingers
and both
joints.

With both joints developed you will find pugnacity, argument, and a didactic mode of expression, boldness of manner and speech, and even malice, especially when to these long-jointed fingers a subject adds a large thumb, which indications generally reveal chicanery, dishonesty, a controversial humor, and a *penchant* towards scandal and mischief-making; the latter particularly when the fingers terminate in short nails.

37.
Large, medium, and small hands.

Thus, to recapitulate: A large hand indicates a love and appreciation of details and minutiæ; a medium-sized hand denotes comprehension of details *and* power of grasping a whole; whilst very small hands betray always the instincts and appreciation of synthesis.

38.
Differences
between
large and
small-handed
subjects.

The large-handed subject will have things small in themselves, but exquisitely finished, whilst the small-handed subject desires the massive, the grand, and the colossal. Artists in horology have always large, whilst the designers and builders of pyramids and colossal temples have always small, hands. In Egyptian papyri and hieroglyphic inscriptions the smallness of the hands of the persons represented always strikes one at first sight.

39.
Handwritings.

In like manner people with small hands always write large, whilst people with large hands always write [naturally] small.

40.
Medium
hands.

Thus it will be seen that it is only medium-proportioned hands that possess the talents of synthesis *and* of analysis, the power of appreciating at the same time the mass, and the details of which it is constituted.

CHAPTER IV.

The Fingers Generally.

THE three phalanges of the fingers have also their significa- **41.** *The three phalanges.* tions. Thus, the first phalanges of the fingers represent the intuitive faculties, the second phalanges represent the reasoning powers, and the third or lowest phalanges represent the material instincts. Thus, therefore, if the third phalanges are relatively the largest, and are thick and full by comparison with the others, the prevailing instincts will be those of sensuality and of luxury; if the second phalanges are the most considerable, a love of reason and reasoning will be the mainspring of the life, whilst with a high development of the first phalanges the intuitive and divine attributes will be the prevailing characteristics of the subject.

Thus, it will be seen, the joints seem to form, as it were, walls **42.** *Effect of the joints.* between the worlds; the joint of philosophy and of reason di- viding the phalanx of intuition and instinct from the phalanx of reason and knowledge; and the joint of material order form- ing the boundary betwixt the reasoning faculties and the world of materialism.

From what has gone before it will be comprehended that thick **43.** *Thick fingers.* fingers will always denote a love of ease and luxury; but also, unless the hand is hard, the subject will not seek and require luxury; he will only enjoy and appreciate it when it comes in his way.

When the fingers are twisted and malformed, with short nails, **44.** *Twisted fingers.* and only the elementary lines [those of head, heart, and life] are visible in the hand, it is almost infallibly the sign of a cruel and tyrannical disposition, if not of a murderous instinct ; but if these twisted fingers are found on an otherwise good hand the deduction to be made will only be that of a mocking and annoying disposition.

45.
Stiff and
hard hands.
If a hand is stiff and hard, opening with difficulty to its full extent, it betrays stubbornness of character.

46.
Fingers turning back.
People whose fingers have a tendency to turn back, being supple and elastic, are generally sagacious and clever, though inclined to extravagance, and always curious and inquisitive.

47.
Fingers
fitting into
one another
or not.
The fingers fitting closely together without interstices between them denote avarice, whereas if there are considerable interstices and chinks between them which show the light through when the hand is held between the eye and the light, it is a sign [like the turning back of the fingers] of inquisitiveness.

48.
Transparent
fingers.
Smoothness and *transparency* of the fingers betray indiscretion and loquacity.

49.
Ball at the
finger tips.
Whatever may be the formation of the fingers, the type to which they belong, or the other conditions of the hand, if a little fleshy ball or knob be found on the face of the first phalanx it is a sign of extreme sensitiveness and sensibility, of tact [from the dread of inflicting pain upon others], and of taste [which is the natural heritage of a nature so gifted].

It may be noted, also, in this place that there are certain indications to be read in the greater or less length and development of each separate finger ; but this is noticed further on under the heading of the Cheirognomy of the Individual Fingers.

CHAPTER V.

The Finger Tips.

THE first [or exterior] phalanges of the fingers of a hand present four principal formations. They are either "*Spatulate*," *i.e.*, the tip of the finger is broad and flat, or club-shaped, like the "spatule" with which a chemist mixes his drugs; "*Square*," *i.e.*, the tip of the finger, instead of being round and cylindrical and curved over the top, is flat upon the tip, and so shaped that a transverse section of the tip would present the appearance of a square, at least as regards three sides thereof [the inside of the finger tip is in almost all cases curved]; "*Conic*," *i.e.*, the tip is cylindrical and rounded over the top like a thimble ; or "*Pointed*," *i.e.*, the finger ends in a more or less extended circular point—and each of these forms has such marked and different characteristics as almost to constitute types by themselves. [With certain concomitant signs they do constitute the Types of Cheirognomy which will be fully considered in a future sub-section ; but it seems right here to notice the particular instincts indicated by each one in particular.]

50.
The four principal formations.

If your fingers terminate in a spatule your first desire will be for action, activity, movement, locomotion, and manual exercise ; you will have a love of what is useful, physical, and reasonable ; yours will be the appreciation of things from the utilitarian point of view, love of animals, and inclination for travel, war, agriculture, and commerce. You will interest yourself principally in the things of real life—physical and mechanical force, calculation, industry, applied sciences, decorative art, and so on.

51.
Spatulate fingers.

52.
Jointed or smooth spatulate fingers

And here [to recede a little] you must take into consideration what we said about the joints, understanding that the subject with spatulate *knotty* fingers will develop and pursue the propensities of the spatulate finger tip by reason, calculation, and knowledge, as opposed to the subject with spatulate *smooth* fingers, who will develop the same characteristics by spontaneity, by impulse, by rapid locomotion, and by inspiration. Thus, if your fingers terminating in spatule have the joints developed you will excel in *practical* science and *scientific* mechanics [such as statics, dynamics, navigation, architecture, and the like]. And the tendencies of this spatulate formation of the finger tips are the more accentuated if you add to them a large thumb and firm hands.

53.
Square fingers.

If your finger tips are square your prevailing characteristics will be symmetry and exactitude of thought and habit. You will have a taste for philosophy, politics, social science and morals, languages, logic, geometry [though you will probably only study them superficially]. You will admire dramatic, analytic, and didactic poetry, and you will require and appreciate metre, rhythm, construction, grammar, and arrangement in literature, whether poetic or otherwise, and your admiration in art will be for the defined and conventional. You will have business capacity and respect for authority, combined with moderate but positive ideas. You will incline to discovery rather than to imagination, to theory and rhetoric rather than to practical action.

54.
Tidiness.

You will admire order and tidiness, but unless your fingers have the joints developed, you will not practise the tidiness you admire—*i.e.*, you will arrange things that are visible, but your drawers and cupboards will be in confusion.

55.
Smooth and jointed square fingers.

Of course, as before, the distinctions of the knotty and the smooth fingers apply to this formation of the finger tips ; the former being always the more sincere and the more trustworthy—

the more ready to put their theories into practice. As we shall presently see [204], a high development of the joints, combined with a large thumb, will give to these square-tipped fingers the most fanatical red-tapeism, regularity, and self-discipline.

Thus it will be easily comprehended that between the spatulate and the square finger tips there are great distinctions, the principal being those of simplicity as opposed to politeness, and of freedom as contrasted with elegance.

56. Spatulate and square finger tips.

Amongst musical people the most thorough theoretical musicians have square fingers, by reason of the amount of rhythm and symmetrical exactitude required. Brilliant execution and talent as an instrumentalist are always accompanied by spatulate fingers [which are *not*, as so many people imagine, the *result* of instrumental practice, but of the temperament which makes that practice a pleasure], whilst singers [who are essentially melodists] have nearly always conical and sometimes pointed fingers.

57. Musical fingers.

Again, if your fingers terminate conically, your whole instinct will be artistic. You will love art in all its branches, and adore the beautiful in the actual and visible form ; you will be enthusiastic, and inclined to romance and social independence, objecting to stern analysis ; your greatest danger is that of being carried away into fantasy.

58. Conical fingers.

If these fingers have either or both joints developed, you will have more moral force, and will be able to keep your more unruly instincts in control. And, as we shall see presently, the tendencies of this conical formation of the finger tips are the more accentuated if the subject have also soft hands and a small thumb. This remark also applies to the pointed formation of the finger tip next below noticed.

59. Conic jointed fingers.

When fingers of these formations [the conic and the pointed] are gifted with a large thumb, their instinctive art will expand itself logically and methodically, almost as if the finger tips were square.

60. Effect of the thumb.

2

61.
Pointed fingers.

And, lastly, suppose your fingers take the form of a cone, drawn out even to pointedness, yours will be exclusively the domain of ideality, contemplation, religious fervor, indifference to worldly interests, poetry of heart and soul, and yearning for love and liberty, cultivation [even to adoration] of the beautiful in the æsthetic abstract rather than in the visible and solid.

62.
Effect of pointedness.

Whatever may be the type, formation, or conditions of a hand, a pointed formation of the finger tips will denote impressionability of the subject. This formation [like the others] will be considered at greater length under the heading of the type to which it particularly belongs.

63.
The four formations.

These are the four principal formations of the finger tips, concerning which space renders it impossible, and the intelligence of the average reader renders it unnecessary, to go further at the present time.

64.
Amorphous finger tips.

If the fingers cannot be classed under any of these formations, but have their tips absolutely shapeless, and consequently irresponsibly ugly and malformed, such a hand is that of a person whose intellect is weak, and whose individuality is practically *nil.*

65.
Excess of formations.

It must be borne in mind that *exaggeration* or *excess* of any form denotes a diseased condition of the instincts indicated, by reason of their too high development.

66.
Excessive pointedness.

Thus, an exaggerated pointedness is apt to be the result of impossible and fanatical romanticism, foolhardiness, and imprudence, exaggeration of imagination, which develops into lying, and particularly into affectation and eccentricity of manner.

67.
Excess of squareness.

Fingers too square show fanatical love of order and method in the abstract, servile submission to conventionality, and to self-prescribed and otherwise regulated ordinances.

Exaggerated spatulation of the fingers indicates tyranny [especially in the thumb], perpetual hurry, restlessness, and discontent with one's fellow creatures.

68.
Excessive spatule.

These excesses of formation are also much influenced by the development or want of development of the thumb [92–93 and 97–98].

69.
Effect of the thumb upon excesses.

CHAPTER VI.

The Hairiness of the Hand.

To leave nothing connected with the hand unconsidered, the greater or less amount of hair found thereon must also engage our attention.

70.
Hairy hands and smooth hands.

A hand the back of which is very hairy betokens inconstancy, whilst a quite hairless and smooth hand denotes folly and presumption. A slight hairiness gives prudence and love of luxury to a man; but a hairy hand on a woman always denotes cruelty.

71.
Hairy thumbs and fingers.

Hair upon the thumb [according to the *Sieur de Peruchio*] denotes ingenuity; on the third or lower phalanges of the fingers only, it betrays affectation, and on all the phalanges, a quick temper and choleric disposition.

72.
Absence of hair.

Complete absence of hair upon the hands betokens effeminacy and cowardice.

CHAPTER VII.

The Color of the Hands.

IF the hands are continually white, never changing color [or only doing so very slightly] under the influences of heat or of cold, they denote egoism, selfishness, and a want of sympathy with the joys and sorrows of others.

73.
Constantly
white hands.

Le Sieur de Peruchio observes, very truly, that in cases such as those of soldiers, of servants, and of work people, whose daily occupations must necessarily alter and affect the coloration of their hands, the colors cannot be relied upon as a certain indication of the temperament; but in the case of women and of persons whose sedentary habits, whose light occupations, or whose care of their hands tends to preserve them in their normal and natural colors and conditions, the following data may with confidence be gone upon:

74.
Persons
whose colorations are significant.

Redness of the skin denotes sanguinity and hopefulness of temperament; yellowness denotes biliousness of disposition; blackness, melancholy; and pallor, a phlegmatic spirit.

75.
Red, yellow,
and dark
hands.

Darkness of tint is always preferable to paleness, which betrays effeminacy; the best color being a decided and wholesome rosiness, which betokens a bright and just disposition.

76.
Preferable
tint.

CHAPTER VIII.

The Thumb.

77.
Importance
of the
thumb.

THE thumb is by far the most important part of the hand, both cheirognomically and practically speaking, for without it the hand would be comparatively [if not absolutely] powerless, and in it the cheirosophist looks for the indications of the two greatest controlling powers of the human system—will and logic.

78.
D'Arpen-
tigny.

" *The hand denotes the superior animal,*" said D'Arpentigny, " *the thumb individualizes the* MAN."

79.
The divisions
of the thumb.

The thumb is divided into three parts—the root [or Mount of Venus], which will be considered fully in a future chapter belonging more especially to cheiromancy pure and simple ; the second phalanx, which is that of logic ; and the first [or nailed] phalanx, which is the seat of the will. Thus it betrays the whole hand, and interprets the direction in which its indicated aptitudes have been, or are being, developed ; for will, reason, and passion are the three prevailing motors of the human race.

80.
The phalanx
of logic and
of will.

The second phalanx indicates our greater or less amount of perception, judgment, and reasoning power ; the first by its greater or less development indicates the strength of our will, our decision, and our capacity for taking the initiative.

81.
The upper
phalanx
weak.

If the first phalanx is poor, weak, and short, it betrays feebleness of will, want of decision and promptitude in action, unreliability and inconstancy, readiness to accept other people's opinions rather than to act upon one's own ; doubt, uncertainty, and indifference.

When a subject has such a thumb as this, and is at the same time devoted to any particular person or cause, or heroic in his action on any particular emergency, his devotion and heroism are spontaneous and sudden [*i.e.*, they are emotional], not premeditated or lasting.

82.
Heroism of a weak thumb.

If with a weak phalanx of will, such as this, your second phalanx [that of reason and logic] is highly developed, you will be able to give excellent reasons for this want of will and uncertainty of disposition, and, though your reasoning powers are excellent, and the promptings of your common-sense are strong, you lack the will and decision to put your common-sense into practice, and to act boldly on the suggestions of your better judgment.

83.
Weak will and strong logic.

And, conversely, if your first phalanx be long, and your second phalanx be short, you will be quick, impulsive, decided, tenacious of your own opinions [however erroneous they may be], and enthusiastic ; but your own want of logic to subdue and direct your spirit of action and strength of will, renders that will of little use to you, and in point of fact you tend toward unreasoning obstinacy.

84.
The upper phalanx strong and the lower short.

A well-developed phalanx of will does often overcome [or at any rate greatly modify] a bad fatality foreshadowed in the palm of the hand.

85.
Power of strong will.

With square fingers and a good line of Apollo, a well-developed first phalanx of the thumb indicates a strong will, tempered and modified by a love of justice, and with a soft hand this decision of character will only be exercised by fits and starts, in consequence of the natural laziness of the disposition.

86.
Strong will with square fingers, etc. With soft hand.

With a highly developed Mount of the Moon, a love of repose and quietude will soothe the activity of a highly developed phalanx of will, which under these circumstances will only show itself by a dictatorial tone in conversation and a domination in manner.

87.
Effect of the Mount of Moon.

If the phalanx is broad, but not particularly long, it betrays obstinacy and unreasonableness, unless with square fingers, when it indicates firmness of judgment and the principles and practice of justice.

88.
Upper phalanx broad.

89.
Excessive broadness of the phalanx of will.

If, besides being the longer, the phalanx of will is excessively broad, even to ugliness, it betrays ungovernable passions and obedience to the promptings of an unreasonable will, obstinacy, furious impulse, and exaggeration in all things. Tyrants, murderers, brutal savages, and the like illustrate greatly this formation, and a man who has this clubbed development of thumb is proportionately to be dreaded as the formation is more or less pronounced.

In a passive hand.

In a hand which is essentially passive, this thumb will denote merely morbid melancholy, especially if the phalanx of logic is short, as the latter, if long, will greatly modify the indications of the form.

90.
Clubbed thumb in a bad hand.

The sign of the clubbed thumb is, however, the more certain when the Mount and Plain of Mars are high and the line of the head is weak. It may, to a great extent, be modified and corrected by a well-developed Mount of Apollo, of Jupiter, or of Venus, or by a good line of heart. With these modifying signs such a subject will rather injure himself in his fits of temper than wilfully do an injury to another.

91.
Upper joint turned back.

When the phalanx of will turns back, as it often does, it indicates extravagance, luxury, and, with other propitious signs, generosity, though an excess of this formation is bad from its unreasoning unthriftiness, which argues a want of moral sense. If, in addition, the Mounts of Jupiter and Mars are high, the extravagance of the subject will be devoted to display and the gratification of his personal vanity ; and, as has been observed before, the same remarks apply [though in a lesser degree] to the fingers, which, if turned back, indicate also extravagance.

92.
Effect of broad thumb.

It must also be noted that broadness of the first phalanx of the thumb [obstinacy] renders any excess of formation found elsewhere in the hand additionally serious and ominous, for it is almost invariably accompanied by a short and small phalanx of logic or reason.

93.
Effect of small thumb.

Therefore, it will be seen that the greater or less development of the various portions of the thumb plays a most important part in

Small

the science of cheirosophy ; you may take it, as a rule, that a small, ill-formed, feeble, or badly developed thumb indicates vacillation of mind, irresolution and want of decision in affairs which require to be governed by reason rather than by instinct or by sentiment.

If the shortness of the second phalanx [logic] shows want of reasoning power ; pointed fingers, a weak line of the head declining upon a high Mount of the Moon, and forked at its extremity, all give unfailing indications of a foolish-mindedness that cannot be counteracted even by a well-developed phalanx of will, or a well-formed line of fortune.

94. Short logic in a weak hand.

Small-thumbed subjects are governed rather by heart, as opposed to large-thumbed subjects, who are governed by head ; the former have more sentiments than ideas, the latter have more ideas than sentiments.

95. Large thumbs and small thumbs.

The bad indications [*i.e.*, the weakness] of a small thumb may be counteracted by a high Mount or Plain of Mars, which will give firmness and decision to the character, as well as calmness and resignation. Another modifying sign is softness of the hand [*i.e.*, laziness], for in this case the subject will not take the trouble to get into mischief [though he lacks the strength of will to resist temptation when it comes in his way].

96. Modifying signs.

With a large thumb, you will be independent and self-reliant, inclining rather to despotism, governing by will rather than by persuasion ; with a small one, you will be reliant on others, easily governed, and wanting in self-confidence, but you will possess, if your fingers be smooth [*no matter what their termination*], the instincts, the natural tendencies [undeveloped though they may be], of art.

97. Effect of large thumb and of small thumb. With smooth fingers.

So in the same way, he who is poetic or artistic by reason of his smooth, conic fingers, is the more certainly so if he have a small thumb ; whilst he who is exact and scientific, by reason of his square or knotted fingers, will be the more so if he have also a large thumb.

98. Small thumb on artistic hand. Large thumb on scientific hand.

CHAPTER IX.

The Consistency of the Hands.

98a.
Indications.

ANOTHER great class difference which exists among hands is that of consistency. That is to say, of two hands outwardly the same, one may be so firm as to be hard, and the other may be so soft as to be flabby, and the great distinction thus indicated is, that soft hands betray a quiet temperament, inclining to laziness, and reaching even to lethargy, whilst hard hands indicate an energetic longing for action and a love of hard physical or manual labor. These differences show themselves chiefly in the way in which the different subjects undertake their work.

99.
Soft and hard hands. Artists.

The soft hand has more poetry in its composition than the hard. Thus, an artist with hard hands will paint things real and actual rather than things ideal, and his pictures will be more active and manly than those of a softer-handed artist, who will paint the images of his fancy, and whose works will show greater soul, greater diversity, and more fantasy.

100.
Hard and soft spatulate hands.

Again, a spatulate subject with hard hands will engage in active exercises, athletics and the like, whilst the similar but softer-handed subject prefers gentler exercise, and prefers to watch others engaging in active occupations; the former will get up early and work hard, whilst the latter will get up later, though when up he will work as hard, or take great interest in seeing others work as hard.

101.
Soft hands.

Again, people with soft hands have always a love of the marvellous, being more nervous, more impressionable, more imaginative than those with hard hands. A *very* soft hand has to a still greater degree developed this fascination for the strange and uncanny, being rendered additionally superstitious by their bodily laziness, which keeps their minds active. The tendency is still more pronounced if the fingers are pointed.

On the other hand, a *soft* spatulate subject, *by reason of his desire* for movement, is always eager to search and experimentalize in the marvellous ; discoveries in the occult sciences are generally made by people with pointed fingers, but these discoveries are always followed up by people with soft spatulate hands.

102.
Soft spatulate hands.

In like manner a very hard hand will be superstitious from want of intellect to make him otherwise, and the tendency will be the more accentuated if the subject have also pointed and smooth fingers.

103.
Very hard hands.

But if a soft hand have a long phalanx of will, the subject, though naturally lazy, will discipline himself, and often compel himself to do work which is distasteful to him.

104.
Influence of the thumb.

I call attention to the circumstance that, as we increase in years and our intellects get weaker, we are apt to take to hard manual labor, such as gardening, carpentering, and the like ; it will be observed that at the same time our hands get firmer, even to hardnesss, and this before natural decay renders them parchmenty and bony. We become more philosophic, and less credulous, more logical, and less romantic, as with age our joints thus develop. I have before alluded [25] to the fact that joints may develop in a smooth hand, as a result of intellectual and scientific cultivation.

105.
Hardness of the hands in age.

Soft hands are often more capable of tenderness and affection than true love ; but hard hands are generally the more capable of true love, though less prone to demonstrative tenderness and affection.

106.
The affections.

To be perfect, a hand should be firm without hardness, and elastic without being flabby ; such a hand only hardens very slowly with

107.
The perfect consistency.

age, whereas an already very firm hand often becomes extremely hard. Smoothness, and a gentle firmness of the hand, in youth, betoken delicacy of mind, whilst dryness and thinness betray rudeness and insensibility.

108.
Hard hands
are like spat-
ulate hands.
A hard hand has, by its hardness, many of the instincts of the spatulate, whatever may be its exterior formation. For instance, it can bear hardships and privations before which a soft-handed sub ject would succumb. It also likes the life of constant effort and struggle, so distasteful to the soft, and so welcome to the spatulate hand.

109.
Excessive
hardness.
It must be also noted that an *exceedingly* hard hand always denotes unintelligence, and if a short phalanx of logic is superadded thereto, the activity of the hand will be ill directed in the pursuit of pleasures and other affairs useless to the owner of the hand.

CHAPTER X.

The Aspect of the Hand.

THE aspect of the hand must also be taken into consideration, in connection with the consistency. Thus, a soft *wrinkled* hand shows impressionability and uprightness of soul, and a wrinkled *hard* hand is that of a person who is pugnacious, irritating, and teasing, especially if the nails be short [146-148].

The *back* of the hand lined and wrinkled always indicates benevolence of mind and sensitiveness of soul.

A hand of good firm consistency, having the joint of order [the second] well developed, with a long phalanx of logic, is an almost invariable indication of good fortune, which is well merited, well striven for, and therefore thoroughly realized.

People of sedentary occupations generally have soft hands, and are generally the most republican in their creeds, because their bodies being quiet, their brains are the more active. These soft-handed republicans are those who rave at their followers and harangue the mob with the premeditated verbiage of experimental incendiarism, whilst the hard-handed republicans are those who organize, who act, and who devote all their energies to the attainment of the objects which their pointed fingers prompt them to strive for.

The man with the firm, strong hands and the developed Mount of Venus is the man who will exert himself to amuse others with feats of grace and of agility ; who will romp with children, and work hard to contribute his share to the general harmony.

115.
Softness
during ill-
ness.

During an illness, a hand which is naturally inclined to be hard will often become temporarily soft, regaining its natural hardness when the ordinary habits of life are resumed. It has been argued from this, that the indications afforded by chirognomy are unstable and unreliable ; but, on the other hand, it is a most interesting fact in support of the science, for the enforced laziness during the time of illness produces in the hand the cheirognomical sign of laziness, and proves that a temporary abandonment of its characteristic employments by a hand will cause it to conform cheirognomically to the indication of the newly acquired (though enforced) course of life.

CHAPTER XI.

The Cheirognomy of the Individual Fingers.

THERE is also to be considered a separate cheirognomy of each individual finger, which must particularly be studied in reading the indications of a *mixed* hand.

Thus, if the first finger [or index] is long, it indicates pride and contemplation; if it is short, it indicates activity and impulse; if it is very long [*i.e.*, as long as the second or middle finger], it indicates a sense of luxury even to sensualism, love of pleasure and comfort rather than of art, combined with an indiscriminating arrogance and egoism which is ashamed of poor relations or associates, if surprised in their company.

116.
The first finger.

A long and pointed first finger betrays religious exaltation. If it is longer than the second finger, it denotes that the life is ruled by ambition or [if the hand is good in its other developments] by religion.

117.
Very long index.

If the first [or nailed] phalanx is long, it denotes religion and intuition; if the second [or middle] phalanx is long, it indicates ambition; and if the third [or lowest] phalanx is long, it betrays pride and love of domination.

118.
The phalanges of the first finger.

If, whilst of normal length, the finger is pointed, the subject has intuition and religious instincts. If the mount at the base of the finger is highly developed, and all the fingers are smooth, we generally find a tendency to ecstasy and mysticism. The intuition of the pointed forefinger applies itself, as a rule, to the

119.
Pointed with a developed mount.

contemplation and perfection of the qualities shown by the formations of the other fingers and the rest of the hand.

120.
Square
index.

If it is square, we find a love of and a search after truth.
Such a subject will seek to discover truth from natural [not oc-
cult] sources of information.   He will have a love of landscape
painting in art, whilst, with a good development of the Mount
of Jupiter, he will have tolerance and reason in religion.

121.
Spatulation
of the index.

A spatulate termination to this finger [fortunately a very
rare form] indicates, as a rule, intense mysticism and error,
especially in a smooth-fingered hand.

122.
The second
finger. Spat-
ulated or
twisted.

If the second [or middle] finger is highly developed and flat
[*i.e.*, inclined to spatulation] it indicates sadness, fatalism, a
morbid imagination, and melancholy. [If it is twisted, it is said
to be a sign of murderous instincts and inclination.]

123.
Pointed
second
finger.

This finger is seldom pointed ; but when it is so, the point
modifies the sad and morbid influence which is the inseparable
evil of the development and conditions of this finger, producing
callousness and frivolity in place of morbidity and moroseness.
This result is more striking if the hand bears also a small thumb.

124.
Square mid-
dle finger.

If the finger is square, the character of the subject becomes
grave in proportion to the greater or lesser accentuation of the
square formation of the finger.

125.
Spatulation
of the mid-
dle finger.

The spatulate is the most natural and ordinary termination
for this finger, giving it activity of imagination, and a morbid
fancy in matters relating to art, science, and literature.

126.
The pha-
langes of
the second
finger.

If on this finger the first phalanx is long, it betokens sadness and superstition; *very* long, it betrays a morbid desire for
death, and, in a weak hand with a small thumb, a horrible
temptation to suicide.   If the second phalanx is long by comparison with the others, it denotes love of agriculture and mechanical occupations, or, if the joints are prominent, mathematics and

the exact sciences. If the fingers are smooth, the development of this second phalanx will give a talent for occult science. Lastly, if the third phalanx is long and large, it denotes avarice.

If the finger incline at the tip towards the first finger, the fatalism indicated thereby is dominated, and to some extent modified, by pride and self-confidence. If it incline towards the third [or middle] finger, this same fatalism is dominated by art.

127. Middle finger inclined towards the third or first.

If the third [or ring] finger is as long as the first, it shows artistic taste, and a desire and ambition to become celebrated and wealthy through artistic talent. If it is as long as the second finger, however, it indicates a gambler, or a person who is foolhardy and rash, especially when the Mount of Mercury is developed. When a hand is otherwise good and strong, this length of the third finger merely indicates a love of adventure and enterprise, especially if the finger tips are spatulate. If the finger is longer than the second or middle finger, it indicates that the instinct and talent for art will triumph over the fatality which will place obstacles in its way and try to impede its progress.

128. The third finger.

If the tip of this finger is pointed, it denotes intuition in art ; but if all the other fingers present different formations of the tips, it will indicate frivolity and levity of mind.

129. Pointed third finger.

A square-tipped third finger will seek for positivism, research and reason in art, and, with the third or lowest phalanx large, a love of wealth.

130. Square third finger.

A spatulate termination to the finger will denote love of action and movement in art, battles, struggles, animated scenes, and representations of them. Such subjects generally make good actors, elocutionists, and orators.

131. Spatulation of the third finger.

If the finger is amorphic and shapeless at its extremity, it denotes positivism of mind and commercial talent and instinct. If the finger is short, whilst the rest of the hand is decidedly

132. Shapelessness or shortness of the third finger.

artistic, the talent for art will be there, but it will indicate a mercenary pursuit of art for the sake of its emoluments and rewards.

133.
The phalanges of the third finger.
The first [or outer] phalanx long, shows great artistic feeling ; the second highly developed, denotes reason and industry in art and the love of those qualities ; the third phalanx dominating the others, betrays love of form and conventionality, vanity in art, and a strong desire for wealth.

134.
The joints of the third finger.
The development of the first [or upper] joint will give to this finger research and love of perfection and finish in art, whilst a prominence of the second [or lower] joint will indicate a love and appreciation of riches.

135.
The fourth finger.
If the fourth [or little] finger is long [*i.e.*, reaching to the middle of the nailed phalanx of the middle finger] it indicates a search after knowledge, a love of education, and a desire to perfect oneself in all kinds of learning. Such a subject will gather quickly the principia of a science, and [from the eloquence and powers of expression, denoted by a development of this finger] can discourse and converse with ease on any subject he has ever taken up. If the finger is as long as the third itself, the owner of the hand will be a philosopher and a savant, unless the whole hand is bad, when this formation denotes cunning and ruse. In the rare cases where the little finger is so long as to reach the top of the second finger, the indication is that the love of science will dominate every fatality of the life, and will surmount every obstacle which may be thrown in his way. If, on the other hand, the finger is very short, it betokens a very quick perception and power of grasping things and reasoning them out with rapidity.

136.
Pointed fourth finger.
A pointed little finger indicates intuition in applied and occult sciences, perspicacity, cunning, and eloquence, which can be brought into requisition to discourse about the veriest nothings. Such sub-

jects make by far the best "after-dinner speakers" and complimentary orators.

Squareness of this finger tip denotes reason in science, love of research and discovery, combined with logic, good sense, and facility of expression when there is need for it.

137. Square little finger.

A spatulation of the little finger gives movement, agitation, and often fantasy in science, fervid and moving eloquence, with a strong aptitude and talent for mechanics. If the rest of the hand is bad, this spatulated formation of the finger tips will indicate theft.

138. Spatulation of the little finger.

If the first phalanx is long, we find love of science and eloquence; when the second phalanx is the longest of the three, we find industry and commercial capacity; and, with a development of the third, we get cunning, cleverness, perspicacity, and lying.

139. The phalanges of the fourth finger.

Prominence of the first joint indicates research in science, and often divination; the salience of the second betrays research and industry in business and commercial skill and aptitude.

140. The joints of the fourth finger.

CHAPTER XII.

The Habitual Actions and Natural Positions of the Hands.

140a.
Cheirology.

IN arriving at an estimate of a character by the application of cheirosophy, there are also to be considered the habitual actions of the hands and the natural positions into which they unconsciously place themselves when in a state of repose. This branch of the science of Cheirosophy has been treated as a distinct science under the name of Cheirology. At present, however, a few of the elementary rules of this branch cannot fail to be of use and interest to the student of Cheirosophy, as being in a high degree germane to the considerations wherewith we are in this volume occupying our attention.

141.
Closed hands and open hands.

To keep the hands always tightly closed denotes secretiveness, and not unfrequently a tendency to untruth. To keep them closed in this manner even when walking betrays timidity and avarice, whilst to carry the hands continually open indicates liberality and openness of disposition.

142.
Carelessness.

To let the hands hang carelessly and loosely by the sides betokens laziness, restlessness, and often a suspicious disposition.

143.
Agitation and quiescence.

If in walking you keep the hands clasped, swinging them to and fro, it shows promptness and impetuosity of character, whilst to keep the hands motionless by the sides betrays dignity and reserve. To keep them absolutely and studiously impassive denotes vanity, conceit, and often falsehood.

144.
The fingers tapping together.

If when the body is at rest the fingers are constantly tapping together, it denotes lightness, dreaminess, and fantasy. If they beat together strongly, it indicates promptitude and decision of opinion ;

whilst, if they tremble, it usually denotes [unless the subject is nervous and highly strung, when it is a natural consequence] folly and often want of principle.

Gaule points out the fact that "the often clapping and folding of the handes note covetous, and their much moving in speech loquacious"; two indications which, though correct, partake rather too much of the nature of truisms.

145.
Gesticulations in speech.

CHAPTER XIII.

The Finger Nails.

146.
Short and broad nails.

IF the nails are short and broad rather than long, with the skin growing far up them, the subject will be pugnacious, critical in disposition, and fond of domination in matters relating to himself and his surroundings ; in fact, he will be imbued with a spirit of meddlesomeness.

147.
Short-nailed women.

With short nails, a woman whose line of heart is small, whose head line is straight and inclined to turn up towards the little finger, whose Mount of Mercury [363] is flat and covered with lines, and whose Mounts of Moon and of Mars are high, with the joints of the finger plainly visible, will be, undoubtedly of the kind of a woman who is known as "a virago." The above are all the signs of harshness and quarrelsomeness in a woman, and the possession of short nails accentuates the certainty of the indications.

148.
Good indications of short nails.

Short nails denote sharpness, quickness of intellect, and perspicacity—with a good line of head, they indicate administrative talent; with a good line of Apollo they indicate irony and badinage.

149.
More indications of short nails.

Short-nailed subjects make the best journalists, by reason of their love of criticism and readiness to engage in any dispute or contention. On a good-natured and happy hand, or in a lazy hand, short nails denote a spirit of mockery and of good-humored sarcasm, frivolity, criticism, and contradiction.

150.
Bitten nails.

It goes almost without saying that when the nails are short from the habit of biting them, they indicate nervousness, abstraction, subject to fits of melancholy, a worrying disposition and continual irritation.

White and shining, soft in texture, with a tendency to pinkness, by reason of their transparency and of a normal and well-proportioned length, the nails indicate a good spirit, delicacy of mind, sensitiveness, tact, and good taste.

151. White smooth nails.

Nails that are both short and pale betoken falsehood and cunning, and a weak physical and moral nature.

152. Short and pale.

Long-nailed subjects are calmer in temper and more gentle than those with short nails ; they are less critical and more impressionable and are of an artistic nature.

153. Long nails.

Nails that are long and thin and very much curved across the finger show a tendency to throat and lung troubles, and this is more accentuated when the nail is heavily ribbed or fluted.

154. Long curved nails.

Nails that are very thick, long and bent, are indicative of a nature inclined to be cruel and unchaste.

155. Long thick nails.

Nails that are of medium length and width and having a bluish tint, denote the circulation of the blood to be at fault, and such subjects will be found to be extremely nervous.

156. Nails with bluish tint.

A branch of Chiromancy, known by the name of Onychomancy, and treating of the white and dark spots found upon the finger nails, is not introduced in this book, as these indications cannot be substantiated.

157. Spots on the nails.

So much, therefore, for the preliminary Cheirognomic examination of the hand generally, and of its various parts and their conditions in particular. It is not necessary to pursue these analytical distinctions further ; the student of Cheirognomy will easily understand how to apply the modifications indicated by these combined and analyzed indications to the general tendencies and instincts suggested by the type of a hand so as to arrive at a comprehension of the most accurate *nuances* of the character and constitution of his subject.

158. Application of general principles.

SUB-SECTION II.

THE SEVEN TYPES OF HANDS, AND THEIR SEVERAL CHARACTERISTICS.

159.
The seven types.
VIEWED by the light of the science of Cheirognomy, all hands belong either to one of six principal classes, or else to a seventh, which is composed of the hands which cannot be rightly classed in any of the other six. These are determined as follows:

     I. The Elementary Hand.

     II. The Spatulate, or Active Hand.

     III. The Conical, or Artistic Hand.

     IV. The Square, or Useful Hand.

     V. The Knotty, or Philosophic Hand.

     VI. The Pointed, or Psychic Hand.

Mixed hands. To these are added a seventh, which is not so much a type by itself as a combination of several. This class comprises those hands which seem to represent more than one type, and are consequently known in Cheirognomy as

     VII. Mixed Hands.

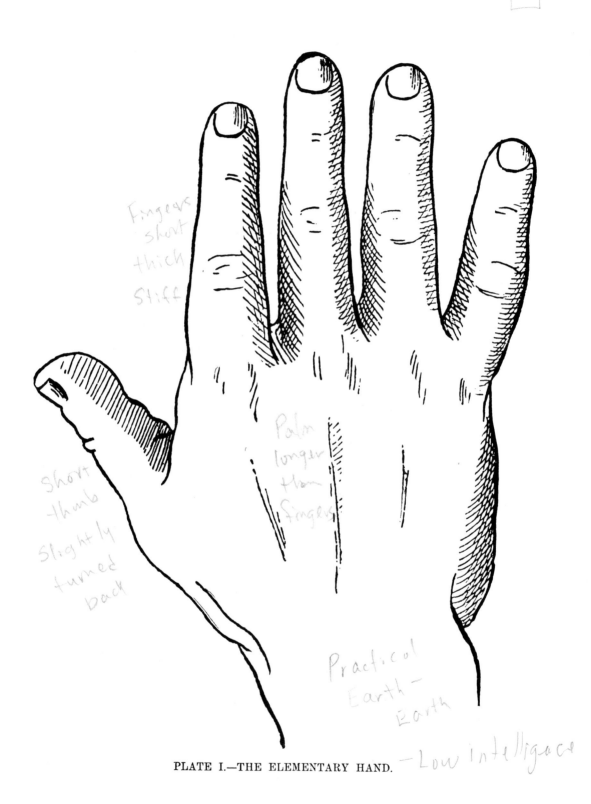

Fingers
short
thick
stiff

Short
thumb
Slightly
turned
back

Palm
longer
than
fingers

Practical
Earth—
Earth

—Low Intelligace

PLATE I.—THE ELEMENTARY HAND.

CHAPTER I.

The Elementary Hand.

THIS is so called because it belongs to the lowest grade of human intelligence, and seems only to be gifted with the amount of intellect requisite to provide the merest necessities of life.

Its outward appearance presents the following features : the fingers are short and thick, wanting in pliability ; the thumb short, often slightly turned back ; and the palm very large, thick, and hard. The palm is, as a general rule, longer than the fingers. These hands very frequently have absolutely no line of Fate [or Fortune] at all.

Such a hand as this betokens a crass and sluggard intelligence, incapable of understanding anything but the physical and visible aspect of things, a mind governed by custom and habit, and not by inclination or originality. Such a character, inaccessible to reason from sheer want of originality of intellect to understand it, is sluggish, heavy, and lazy as regards any occupation beyond its accustomed toil. It has no imagination or reasoning powers, and will only exert itself mentally or physically so as to obtain that which is absolutely necessary to its existence. Thus in war such hands will only fight to defend themselves, and not for glory or honor ; such people fight with a brutish ferocity, but without any attention to the arts of modern warfare. They act by rule and rote, *not* in obedience to their passions or imagination, which are conspicuous by their absence. Such people, having no instinct of cultivation, would regard education as a folly, if not as a crime or as something unholy.

162.
Specimens of
the type.

The Laplanders are the best specimens of this type ; and out of their latitudes the true elementary hand is very seldom found in its pure crass unintelligence, except perhaps among the lower class Tartars and Slavs, who *exist*, rather than *live*, with an existence which is purely negative, dead to any of the higher considerations which make life worth living.

163.
Quasi-
elementary
hands.

Though this type, in its pure state, does not exist among us, still we often see hands with a strong tendency to the elementary form. Such will be noticed among mixed hands, and it will be found that they always bring these coarse and sluggish qualities to interfere with those of the dominant type of the hand.

164.
Powers of
cultivation.

Almost the only charm to which these minds are accessible is that of music [346]. They are generally superstitious, and always ignorant ; and, having no strength of mind, they are stricken most sorely by any grief or disaster which overtakes them.

165.
Contrasting
types.

With the Laps and Slavs as the examples of this type, we may take the Moslems and Hindoos as the contrasting opposites. Among these poetic, cunning, romantic, sensual peoples the elementary hand does not exist, and to perform the degrading and menial offices which are with us performed by hands showing the developments of this type, these Oriental nations have to employ a separate class of low-caste creatures to whose elementary hands such labors do not come amiss.

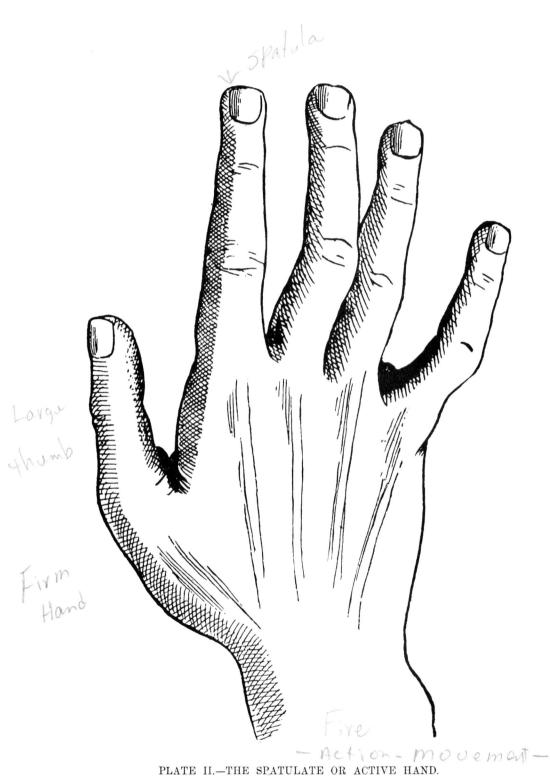

spatula

Large thumb

Firm Hand

Fire

— Action — movement —

Energy —

PLATE II.—THE SPATULATE OR ACTIVE HAND.

CHAPTER II.

The Spatulate, or Active Hand.

THIS is the hand whose fingers have the first [or outer] phalanx terminating more or less in a spatula, and, bearing in mind what has been said in a previous sub-section [97–98] concerning the thumb, it will be easily conceived that this latter must be large to give the true character to the spatulate hand.

The great pronounced characteristics of this type are: action, movement, energy; and, of course, the harder or firmer the hand, the more pronounced will these characteristics be. A man of this type is resolute, self-confident, and desirous of abundance rather than of sufficiency; he will be more active than delicate, more energetic than enthusiastic; in love he will be more constant and faithful [though less tender and affectionate] than the conic or pointed-handed subject, by reason of his want of inclination towards things romantic and poetic.

With a small thumb a spatulate subject will try to do much, but will fail, through want of perseverance, to carry out his intentions, from uncertainty in his course of action. He will voyage, but his voyages will be aimless and objectless; he will be active, but his activity will be futile, and produce no results. These diminutions of the force of the type will, however, be greatly modified if the small thumb be largely composed of a long phalanx of logic, [the second,] which formation will reduce within practicable limits his uncertainty, and quicken the intellect to give a better direction to his activity.

If, with spatulate tips, his fingers be very smooth, he will admire elegance in his surroundings and in the things which conduce to his comfort ; but it will be a fashionable rather than an artistic form of elegance. His will be the love of *reality* in art and energy in its pursuit; he will be fond of horses, dogs, navigation, the science of agriculture, the mechanical arts, the theory of warfare, and the talents of administration and command—in fact, all pursuits where the *mind* directs the activity. In all his active pursuits he will seek inspiration for the motive of his procedure. Such subjects are generally musicians, and when this is so, they are great executants. Such subjects, also, are usually self-centred and essentially egotistical.

People with spatulate hands make the best colonists, because they are only attached to a country for what it produces for them ; they like manual labor and all other forms of activity, being intolerant of insufficiency ; if, therefore, their native land is overcrowded, and the good things of this life are scarce, they are quite satisfied to migrate in search of abundance. They are only very slightly sensual, and are greedy rather than epicurean ; they like travelling about and seeing new places ; being very self-confident, they have no objection to solitude, and are clever at all utilitarian sciences, which enable them to shift for themselves.

A man of the spatulate type admires architecture, but likes it to be stupendous rather than ornate. They are great arithmeticians, and to please them, things must be astonishing and exact, representing a large amount of physical labor. With them the artisan is more considered than the artist ; they appreciate wealth rather than luxury, quantity rather than quality. A town, to suit their views, must be clean, regularly built, substantial, and of business-like appearance.

These subjects will be fond of order and regularity, because of its appearance, and they will arrange and tidy things more from the desire to be *doing* something than from the love of tidiness itself.

Their laws are strict and often tyrannical, but always just ; and their language is forcible rather than ornate. They are brave, industrious, and persevering ; not cast down by trifles, but rather courting difficulties, so as to surmount them. They desire to command, and are intolerant of restraint, unless for their individual good. They are most tenacious of what is their own, and are always ready to fight for their rights.

172. Administration of the type.

People who boast of an ancient lineage, and descent from the feudal barons of the Middle Ages, and show in support of their pretensions a fine, pointed, smooth hand, make a great mistake, for the true old stock of the fighting *ancienne noblesse* are always distinguishable by their spatulate fingers.

173. Hand of the hereditary nobility.

If the spatulate hand has no need to fight, it will hunt, shoot, fence, race, and, in fact, do anything which conveys the impression of, and satisfies their *penchant* towards activity and strife.

174. Occupations of the type.

In religion the spatulate subject desires a belief reasoned out and certain.

175. Religion.

The North American is the embodiment of this spatulate type, with his advanced notions, his industry, perseverance, and cunning ; his economy, caution, and calculation ; and as a result of many of these characteristics, we find the type largely represented in Scotland, far more generally indeed than in England, as a moment's consideration will prove to be natural.

176. Spatulate-handed nations.

It is to the spatulate type, therefore, that we owe nearly all our great men in the world of physical exertion, of active enterprise, and of applied science ; their watchwords being, from first to last—energy, movement, hardihood, and perseverance.

177. Talents of the type.

The excess of this type [*i.e.*, a too highly developed spatulation of the finger tips] will produce a tyrannical desire for action, and a

178. Excess of the formation.

tendency to be constantly worrying and urging other people to increased activity. Such subjects are constantly finding fault, and their freedom of manner and liberty of thought and expression know no bounds. This excess will also give brusquerie and roughness of manner, especially when the Line of Life is thin and red ; but a good Line of Heart and well-developed Mount of Venus will reduce these significations to a rough good-nature.

179.
Perversion of the success of the type.

When a hand whose spatulate developement is thus in excess, has the joints developed and a small thumb, the indication will be that of unsuccessfulness in research and invention, arising from the fact that an excessive activity is perverted by want of will to keep it in check.

180.
Spatulate tips and upper joint.

If this type of hand have the first joint developed, its owner will be endowed with reasoning faculty and independence of rule in his active pursuits. He will be eminently sceptical of tenderness or affection until its existence is proved to him, intolerant of fanaticism, and dead to the charms of imagination and the interests of eccentricity. His will be the talent of politics ; he will object to anything uncomfortable or uncertain ; he will hate poetry and enthusiasm, and will be endowed with an extreme self-confidence. This development will give him a spirit of cohesion to his fellow-men, resistance against innovation, and a love of political freedom of the masses.

181.
Both joints developed.

With *both* joints developed he will combine with his physical energy exact sciences and practical studies ; he will devote himself to all mechanical and constructive arts, navigation, geometry and the like ; he will affect particularly the sciences which regulate the laws of motion or action. Such men make the best inventors and engineers, for the activity of their bodies puts into execution and carries out the suggestions and discoveries of their minds.

182.
Soft spatulate hand.

When a spatulate hand is very soft, the spirit of action will have a powerful enemy in an innate laziness. Such a subject will be a late riser, and a man of sedentary habits ; but will love the spectacle and noise of action and movement. He will like to travel and hear about travels, but he will travel comfortably, preferring to hear and read about the actions and movements of others than to be active and energetic himself.

A subject whose spatulate hands have the first [or upper] joint developed will be constantly forming plans and projects, which will, however, come to nothing, unless the phalanx of will is long in the thumb, in which case he will *make* himself carry out his plans.

183. Soft hand with upper joint developed.

CHAPTER III.

The Conical, or Artistic Hand.

THIS hand is, in its appearance and in the characteristics of the type which it represents, a great contrast to the one whose consideration we have just relinquished.

184.
Its three variations.

It is subject also to three variations of formation and concomitant characteristics which modify the indications of the type as regards the ends to which it works. Firstly, a supple hand with a small thumb and a developed though still medium palm. This hand is drawn invariably to what is actually beautiful in art. Secondly, a large hand, rather thick and short, with a large thumb. This hand is endued with a desire of wealth, grandeur, and good fortune. And, thirdly, a large and very firm hand, the palm highly developed. This formation indicates a strong tendency to sensuality. All three are governed by inspiration, and are absolutely unfit for physical and mechanical pursuits ; but the first goes into a scheme enthusiastically, the second cunningly, and the third with an aim towards self-gratification.

185.
Its appearance.

Hands of this type always present the following form [modified, of course, by the conditions enumerated in the last paragraph]: The fingers, slightly broad and large at the third [or lowest] phalanx, grow gradually thinner, till the tips of the first [or nailed] phalanges terminate in a cone [as in Plate III.]. The thumb is generally small, and the palm fairly developed.

Such a subject will be ruled by impulse and instinct, rather than by reason or calculation, and will always be attracted at once by the

Ruled by impulse & instinct
rather than reason
Loves beauty, rather than usefulness
- freedom lover -
- lover of ease
- moodie

← Conic

Supple

← Broad

Supple
hand

Small
thumb

Palm well
developed

PLATE III.—THE CONICAL OR ARTISTIC HAND.

Air

- Artistic temperament -
- Impulse -   - Love of the beautifull
- egotism -   - Prefers the Ideal to
                       the real -
                     - Beauty in people -

beautiful aspects of life and matter. He will prefer that things should be beautiful rather than that they should be useful. Attracted by ease, novelty, liberty, and anything which strikes his mind as being pleasant, he is at the same time vain, and fearful of ridicule ; enthusiastic, but outwardly humble, and his prime motive powers are enthusiasm and impulse, rather than force or determination. Subject to the most sudden changes of temperament, he is at one moment in the seventh heaven of excitable hopefulness, and the next in the nethermost abyss of intangible despair. Unable to command, he is incapable of obedience. He may be attracted in a given direction, but never driven. The ties of a domestic life are unbearable to him. At heart he is a pure Bohemian. In lieu of ideas he has sentiments. Light-hearted, open-handed, and impulsive, his imagination is as warm as his heart is by nature cold. In speech he gesticulates, and seeks to impress his meaning by movements of the hands, and he generally succeeds in imparting his enthusiasm to those around him. It is a hard-surfaced hand of this type which characterizes the general whose soldiers follow him blindly, who acts on impulse and under excitement for honor and glory, and who leads his men without fear to death or to victory.

186. Proclivities and indications of the type.

If the characteristics of his type are still more developed [*i.e.*, the palm larger, the fingers smoother and more supple ; a small thumb, and the finger tips a more accentuated cone] he is still more the slave of his passions, and he has still less power to hold himself in check. His whole character may be denominated *spirituel.* To him pleasure is a passion, beauty a worship. If he takes up any pursuit he is wild over it. If he makes a friendship, it is an adoration. Never taking the trouble to hate, he never makes enemies. Generous and open-hearted even to extravagance, his purse, which is closed hermetically to his creditors, is always at the service of his friends. He is most sensitive to blame or suspicion, and greatly touched by

187. Accentuation of the type.

4

friendship and kindness. Such subjects will conform to law [so long as it does not interfere with them], because they cannot take the trouble to rebel against it; but they will not brook political despotism which interferes with their comfort, in which cases they will rush enthusiastically to the extremes of republicanism, social-ism, and nihilism.

188.
Evil tend-encies of the type.

Very often in an artistic nature are found only the defects of the type: Sensuality, laziness, egotism, eccentricity, cynicism, dissipation, incapacity for concentration, cunning, falsehood, and exaggeration— a formidable list, truly, but a moment's thought will show how easily they may become the besetting sins of an artistic nature. In these cases the hands are large and very firm, the palm highly de-veloped, the Mount of Venus high, and the third [or lowest] phalanx of the fingers always thick and large.

189.
Affections of the type.

Subjects of the artistic type are not nearly so capable of constancy in love as their square or spatulate brethren and sisters [166], for they are so apt to fall in love on impulse, and without consideration, whereas with the spatulate, true love, [as are all other subjects,] is a matter of reason and calculation. Again, subjects of the artistic type are, to a great extent, incapable of warm, platonic affection,—filial, paternal, or otherwise,—for in all their emotions they seek the pleas-ure of the senses rather than the mental and moral satisfactions of attachment.

190.
The characteris-tics of the type.

Beauty is the guiding principle of these hands, but were the world to be entirely populated by them, want of foresight, folly, splendid poverty, and the fanaticism of form would be universal. The artistic type may, therefore, be summed up thus: Its prevailing characteristics are love of the beautiful, preference of the ideal to the real, intuition, impulse, and egotism.

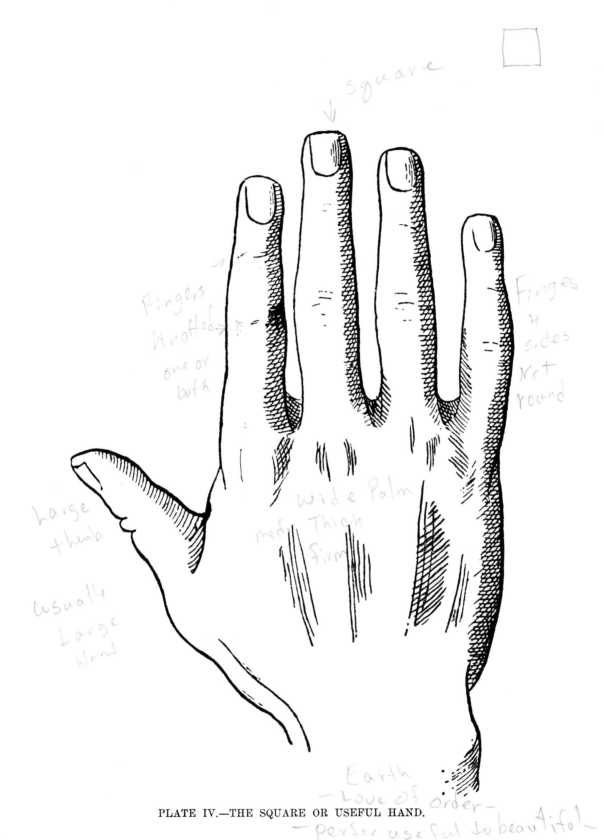

square

Fingers
knotted
one or
both

Finges
4
sides
not
round

Large
thumb

Usually
Large
Hand

Wide Palm
med. Thick
firm

Earth
—Love of order—
—Prefer useful to beautiful

PLATE IV.—THE SQUARE OR USEFUL HAND.

CHAPTER IV.

The Square, or Useful Hand.

THIS hand generally inclines to size rather than to smallness, the size being usually produced by an increased breadth of the hand, the fingers knotted [*i.e.*, with one or both joints developed, generally, in fact, nearly always, the second or lower one], the outer phalanx square [*i.e.*, the fingers throughout their length having four distinct sides, not being rounded, as is the case with an artistic or psychic hand], the thumb rather large, with the root [Mount of Venus] well developed ; the palm of a medium thickness, hollow, and rather firm [*Plate* IV.].

The leading instincts on which this hand founds all its characteristics are perseverance, foresight, order, and regularity. To these hands the useful is far preferable to the beautiful ; their great passion is organization, arrangement, classification, regularity of form and outline, and the acceptation of things prescribed and understood as customary. They like things of a sort to match, and they have essentially the talent of perceiving in things apparently different the points of similarity, and *per contrâ* in things outwardly similar the points of difference. They are great disciplinarians, preferring the good of the community to the welfare of the individual. They are only romantic within the bounds of reason, and are constant in love, more from a sense of the fitness of things than from depth of feeling. They have the greatest aptitude for comforming to the observances of social life, for they are great respecters of persons, and submissive to established authority, from their great love of regularity and order in human affairs.

193.
Square and spatulate types compared.

We find the same submission to authority in the character of subjects of the spatulate type, but with them it arises from another cause. The spatulate subject submits from personal love of his superior, to whom he naturally attaches himself, whilst the square-handed subject submits from admiration of the principles of constituted authority. The dictator must be *powerful* to obtain the allegiance of the spatulate subject; he need only be *properly constituted* to be sure of the allegiance of the square.

194.
Proclivities of the type.

They cherish their privileges, preferring them to complete liberty; and they have a passion for varied experience, which they are always ready to pay for, preferring acquired knowledge to intuitive perception.

195.
Religion.

A *Croix mistique* [591] in a square hand will give it calm and reasonable religion.

196.
Orderliness of the type.

They are slaves to arrangement—that is, they have a place for everything, and everything is in its place; unless their fingers have also the joints developed, it is quite possible [if not probable] that their rooms and cupboards may be outwardly very untidy, but, nevertheless, they always know where everything is. Their books, of which they keep catalogues and indexes, are inscribed with their names and the date of acquisition, and are arranged more in subjects than in sizes, though they love to see them in even sizes as much as possible. They are natty and handy with their fingers, neat and well-brushed in their persons, polite and courteous in their manners, whilst they are great sticklers for the ordinances of etiquette.

197.
Indications of the type.

As a rule, they will only comprehend things as far as they can positively see them, having themselves far too well under control to allow themselves to launch into enthusiasm; they are, therefore, strong disciplinarians, prone to details, fond of minutiæ. Their course of life is regular and pre-arranged, they are punctual, and intolerant of unpunctuality, except when they can regard it as a foil for their own exactness ; for they are always vain even to conceit, though they are always too well bred to obtrude their vanity in its more usual and vulgar forms.   They are graceful in their movements, generally good shots, and good at games and exercises of skill, as opposed to exercises of mere physical strength.

The best musicians [especially harmonists and musical theoreticians] have always delicately squared fingers, with slightly developed joints and small thumbs [702]. **198.** Musicians of the type.

Square-handed people can always govern the expressions of their faces, their language, and their looks ; they are most averse to sudden changes of temperament or circumstance.   Moderate *rangés*, they mistake the perfect for the beautiful ; they cannot bear excitements and " scenes," and they hate when people obtrude their troubles, discomforts, or quarrels upon them.   They dress very quietly, but always very well, and they avoid studiously anything like ostentation, or display in matters of eccentricity, ornament, or jewelry, excepting on fitting occasions, when their magnificence is striking from its good taste. **199.** Manners of the type.

They like poetry to be neat and geometrically perfect, rather than grand or rugged ; they call things by generic rather than by specific or distinctive names, and prefer terms which express the use of a thing rather than its appearance.   They are generally suspicious and quietly cunning, vigilant, and complete masters of intrigue ; they prefer common sense to genius, and social observance to either ; they are often flatterers, and are themselves most susceptible to flattery, ambitious, but quietly and steadily, rather than enthusiastically and obviously so.   They worship talent and cultivation, though without sycophancy ; they are fond of arithmetical calculations, though very often not clever at them themselves, unless their thumbs be large, **200.** Further characteristics of the type.

and the Line of Apollo absent, which are signs which always betray a talent for mathematics. They are good talkers, listeners, and entertainers ; they make many acquaintances, but few friends. They do not require men to be sociable, so much as blind to the faults of themselves and others.

201.
Smooth square fingers.
When the fingers, besides being square, are decidedly smooth, the subject will take poetical views of things material and useful, and will affect the study of moral sciences, philosophy, metaphysics, and the like. He will have the instincts of art, and require truth therein ; in poetry he will require rhythm, form, and period. Such a mind is well regulated, and he will check a natural tendency to enthusiasm.

202.
With declining Line of Head.
The smooth, square hand is one of the cleverest that exist ; love of *truth* in matters which concern itself is one of its first principles, *but*, if the Line of Head come down upon the Mount of the Moon [478], this instinct will often be annulled, especially if the line is forked, but there will always be an order and a method in the chimæras to which such a subject is irresistibly addicted, which gives them a strong semblance of truth.

203.
Upper joint developed.
A square hand, if it has the first joint developed, will have the great advantage over its fellows of the type, of a sincerity, a love of progress and justice which elevates it above the defects of its class. Its calm and cool research after truth will cause it to require reason in matters of art, and object to anything *outré* or unaccustomed. Law and rule are the necessities of its life.

204.
Both joints developed.
If both joints are developed, it will indicate a great love of elegant sciences, of the studies of botany, archæology, history, law, and orthography, geometry, grammar, mathematics, and agriculture. This subject will be aggressively methodical, and will insist upon ticketing, docketing, classifying, arranging everything and upon doing everything according to rule, or to a pre-arranged order.

He will be fond of clearly defined and ascertained studies. [History and politics rather than metaphysics or occult science.] But a small thumb, or a high Mount of the Moon, will give such a subject as this a strange faculty for occultism. At the same time he will have a strongly developed instinct of justice, and is thoroughly trustworthy and true.

205.
With Mount of the Moon.

Good sense, therefore, is the guiding principle of the square type, but, were the world wholly populated by them, fanatical "red-tapeism" and narrow-minded despotism would be universal.

206.
Character of the type.

Excess of this formation will give fanaticism of order and method, despotism in discipline, and narrow-mindedness.

207.
Excess of the type.

A square-fingered hand, to be perfect, should have short nails [argument and self-defence] to defend its love of justice.

It would be easy to continue the interesting subject of the square type to a considerable length, if space would allow it, but we must leave these precise and insincere hands, to turn our attention to another type, which in some respects resembles them, namely, the Knotty, or Philosophic Hand.

208.
The finger-nails.

CHAPTER V.

The Knotty, or Philosophic Hand.

209.
Its divisions.

M. D'ARPENTIGNY divides this type into two classes or sections: One, that of the sensualists, whose ideas are derived from external influences; and the other that of the idealists, whose ideas are evolved from their inner consciousness.

210.
Its appearance.

The appearance of the hands of this type is most distinctive. A large elastic palm, both joints developed, the outer phalanx presenting the mixed appearance of the square and of the conic finger tips. This formation, combined with the development of the first or upper joint, gives the finger tips an oval, clubbed appearance, which is rather ugly, but very characteristic. The thumb is always large, having its two phalanges [those of will and of logic] of exactly the same length, indicating a balancing proportion of will and common sense.

211.
Its characteristics.

The great characteristics indicated by this type of hand are— analysis, meditation, philosophy, deduction, poetry of *reason*, independence, often deism and democracy, and the search after, and love of, the abstract and absolute truth. The development of the joints gives this hand calculation, method, and deduction; the quasi-comic formation of the exterior phalanx gives it the instinct of poetry in the abstract, and beauty in things real; and the thumb gives it perseverance in its metaphysical studies. In all things these subjects desire truth more than beauty, and prefer the meaning of a sentiment to the manner in which it is expressed; thus, their literature is remarkable for its clearness, its utility, and its variety as

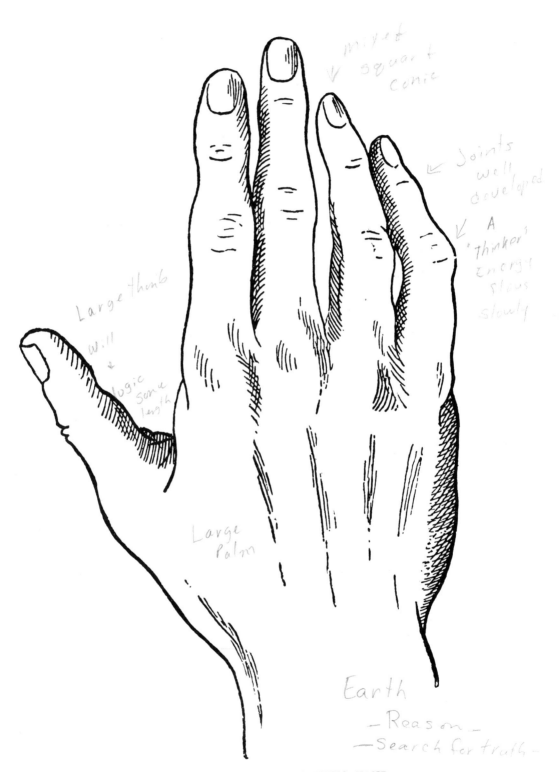

Desire Truth more than beauty
Reason guiding principle

mixed square conic

Joints well developed

A "thinker" energy flows slowly

Large thumb will & logic some leng

Large Palm

Earth
— Reason —
— Search for truth —

PLATE V.—THE KNOTTY OR PHILOSOPHIC HAND.

opposed to that of the square type, which is notable principally for its finish and regularity of style, and they are great lovers and students of the pure sciences—whether moral, physical, æsthetic, or experimental.

Such subjects like to account for everything, to know the reason of everything, whether physical, metaphysical, physiological, or psychic ; their ideas they form for themselves, without caring in the least for those of other people ; their convictions—religious, social, and otherwise—are only acquired as the result of careful analysis and consideration of the questions involved ; love, instinct, faith, are all made subordinate to reason, which is the principle more powerful with them than rule, conventionalism, inclination, or love, except in matters of religion, for their religion is one rather of love and adoration than of fear and conventionality. It is thus that among the subjects of this type we find a large proportion of persons who become known as sceptics of various kinds, for they look upon doubt and scepticism as one of the first necessary evils of life, which will give way to reverence and adoration, and therefore do not in any way worry themselves on this account.

212.
Its religion.

The subjects of the philosophic type do not study detail to the exclusion of entirety, or the individual to the exclusion of the community, but are capable of considering and comprehending the synthesis *and* the analysis of any subject to which they may turn their attention. Therefore, they are tolerant of all forms of rule, seeing at once the good and the bad points of any or every system of government.

213.
Synthesis and analysis.

Forked head line

They are just, [from an intuitive sense of justice and a discriminating instinct of ethics,] unsuperstitious, great advocates of social and religious freedom, and moderate in their pleasures. It is in these respects that they differ so totally from the subordination and conventionalism of square-fingered hands.

214.
Further characteristics.

215.
Philosophic
development
of other
types.

Thus reasoning out everything, the philosophic type constitute almost entirely the vast schools of the Eclectics.   And besides hands which are distinctly of this philosophic type other types may, by the development of joints, attain [as we have seen] attributes of this one.   Thus : a square [or useful] or a spatulate [or active] hand may have its joints developed ; this will give them a love of theorizing and speculating on matters of practice, realty and custom.   In the same way a conic [or artistic] hand, whose joints are developed, will search after truth in matters appertaining to art, and will speculate upon, and analyze the means of attaining the *truly* beautiful.

216.
Small and
large hands.

If the philosophic hand is small, it thinks and reasons from the heart, studying the entireties of matters which present themselves in masses ; if large, and with a proportionate thumb, it thinks and reasons with the head, studying the analysis of those masses, but the result is always the same.

217.
The guiding
principle.

Attained possibly by different means, the end is always identical, and in all things directed by reason, and by common sense, directed by will.   *Reason* is the guiding principle of these hands.

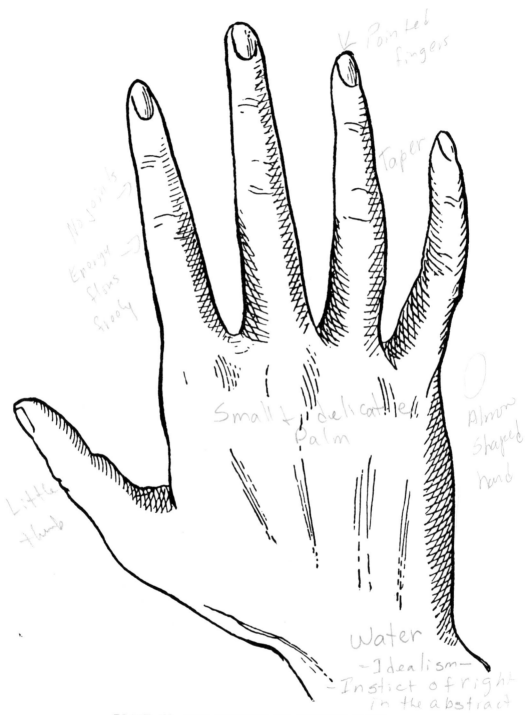

Pointed fingers

Taper

No joints

Knotty Flows Smooth

Small + delicate Palm

Almond shaped hand

Little thumb

Water

—Idealism—
—Instict of right
in the abstract
—love of beauty—

PLATE VI.—THE POINTED OR PSYCHIC HAND.

CHAPTER VI.

The Pointed, or Psychic Hand.

WE have now reached the consideration of the most beautiful and delicate, but, alas! the most useless and impractical type of hand. This hand is but rarely found, but when you do see it, you cannot help remarking it, and will therefore recognize it at once by its description.

218.
Its rarity.

It is very small and delicate, having a thin palm, smooth, fine fingers, long and delicately pointed, or with its joints only just indicated by a very slight swelling. It has generally a pretty little thumb.

219.
Its appearance.

To these subjects belong the domains of the beautiful ideal, the land of dreams, of Utopian ideas, and of artistic fervor; they have the delicacy and true instinct of art of the conic hand, without its bad points, its sensualism, its egotism, and its worldliness. They are guided only by their idealism, by impulse, by their instinct of right in the abstract, and by their natural love and attraction for the beautiful in all things, whether mundane or celestial; bearing the same relation to the philosophic hands that the artistic bear to the useful, the relation of contrast.

220.
Their guiding principle.

These hands never command, for they establish for themselves far too lofty an ideal to care about earthly domination or material interests of any kind; they are incapable of strife or struggles for glory, but, if their instincts of the ideally just are aroused, they will devote themselves even to death in defence of what they consider to be ethically right. Such were the heroes of La Vendée, such were

221.
Their characteristics.

the persecuted followers of Huz, and in such manner is accounted for the devoted enthusiasm of the Moorish and Moslem tribes, who fight like wild beasts for the defence of their faiths, for Allah, his prophet, and the Qur'ân. They will undertake huge forlorn enterprises, but will disdain to embark upon small, practicable expeditions, in quest of some material good.

Idealism.

222.
The gift of prophecy.

[*Desbarrolles*, in calling attention to the fact that they not unfrequently have the gift of prophecy, says that he considers their attributes due to the fact that the absence of joints produces a clear passage for the currents of animal electricity or magnetism to which he considers the gifts of prophecy, presentiment, divination, and even ordinary intuition attributable. He considers that the joints in the fingers of the other types act as obstacles to the passage of "la fluide" [which he believes man to receive (if at all) at his finger tips] to a greater or less degree as those joints are more or less developed, and that to the absence of these joints in the psychic hand their intuition, divination, and presentiments are to be ascribed.]

223.
Artists.

An artist with hands presenting the appearance of a psychic formation will paint subjects of wild romance, but will not seek to paint ideas which convey an impression of *truth.* Such subjects have no instinct of real life, nor are they [as the absence of joints would denote] orderly in themselves, or in their ideas.

224.
Hereditary hands.

As has been stated, these hands are *not* the exclusive inheritance of noble birth ; we find them in all classes of life, from the highest to the lowest, and wherever and whenever they are found, their characteristics are the same—worldly uselessness, with æsthetic perfection and poetry of soul in their highest state of development. Soul is with them the first consideration ; form or treatment is with them subordinate to subject, as is also execution to idea. Amongst all classes they are respected for their very incomprehensibility.

The excess of this type [*i.e.*, when the exaggeration of the pointedness is extremely marked] produces romancers, posturists, fanatics of various kinds, persons prone to fantasies and ecstasies, foolhardiness and deceitfulness, and often mysticism. If the Line of Heart is strong, we find in this case excess of affection, which is carried to an extreme, and affectation of manner.

225. Excessive development of the type.

The luxurious, dreaming Orientals are almost exclusively of this type. Among them we find spiritualists, mediums, and all the so-called "weak-minded" devotees of physical science, who accept all that is told them without investigation or analysis, and are, therefore, the easy prey of "spiritualistic" impostors. In countries where such hands predominate and hold the reins of government, we find that rule is maintained by superstition and by fetichism.

226. Orientals and spiritualists.

These subjects can, however, see beauty and good in every form of rule and government from Autocracy to Republicanism, and in every form of belief from Popery to Positivism. It is the psychic hand that invents a religion, and it is the philosophic, the useful, and the active hands that dissect that religion, and analyze its claims to consideration.

227. Psychic administration and religion.

Such subjects are ruled by heart and by soul; their feelings are acute, their nerves highly strung, and they are easily fired with a wondrous enthusiasm. Theirs are the talents which produce the most inspired poetry; their influence over the masses is extreme, from their power of communicating their enthusiasm to their fellow-men, a power whereby they appeal alike to the most refined and to the most coarse, to the most intellectual and to the most ignorant.

228. Sympathy of the type.

It would take many pages to give these beautiful, useless hands their due. We can only congratulate ourselves that their refining influence exists among us, and that we of the spatulate and square types can work to support them, instead of allowing the world to

229. Value of the type.

crush their beautiful characteristics and dull the keenness of their pure intuition.

230.
Upper joint developed.

If the pointed hand have the first joint developed, the character of the owner of that hand will be changeable, and apt to rush from one extreme to another, from ecstatic enthusiasm to suspicion, scepticism, and levity ; he will be essentially credulous in things savoring of the marvellous and the mystic ; he will be eccentric, and unable to reconcile himself to any prescribed religion ; it is such subjects that become fanatics and religious monomaniacs.

231.
Religion of the type.

They have the inspiration and intuition of truth, with a continual desire to analyze their impulses, and to master their romantic emotions. This often causes them to separate themselves from all recognized forms of belief, and to strike out for themselves new religions to satisfy the romantic instinct of piety, which with them is so strongly developed.

232.
Both joints developed.

With both joints developed, a psychic hand will lose much of its exaltation of character by mingling it with calculation, reason, positivism, and the faculty *of invention ;* at the same time, it cannot complete and develop its inventions and calculations itself, but leaves them unfinished for square and spatulate hands to work out.

233.
Effect of joints.

Such a subject, unless his thumb is large, will be prone to discontentedness, doubt, fear, and dejection ; and also, with a weak hand, will be Utopian and revolutionary in his views from his very instinct of calculation. These jointed hands of the psychic type have often all their spirit and spontaneous impulse annulled or levelled ; their artistic intuitions are spoiled by their instincts of calculation and invention, but *still*, in that calculation and invention the old inspiration and intuition will make itself felt and apparent.

234.
Hard hands.

Sometimes a hand of the pointed type is hard. This will betoken an artistic use of strength, as in the case of dancers, jugglers, acrobats, and the like.

CHAPTER VII.

The Mixed Hand.

It is here that the task of the cheirognomist becomes most difficult, calls forth all his intuitive perception and skill of analysis, and gives him the greatest difficulty in putting his perceptions into words.

The mixed hand is that one of which the shape is so uncertain as to resemble, even to possibility of confusion, more than one type. Thus, an artistic hand may be so marked in its conicality as to become almost psychic; a square hand may be confounded with a spatulate; or, having developed joints and a quasi-conic tip, may be mistaken for a philosophic, and so on *ad infinitum*. In such cases the cheirosophist must so combine, mentally, the tendencies of both types represented, as to arrive at a true analysis of the character of the subject under examination.

235.
Its constitution.

In reading the indications afforded by these mixed hands, you will do well to bear very carefully in mind the cheirognomy of the individual fingers.

236.
Difficulty of interpretation.

To the mixed hand belongs the talent of dealing between people as merchants or administrators of justice. They succeed best in intermediary arts—*i.e.*, those of a plastic, regular, and acquired description, such as illumination, carving, heraldry, or decoration. A man endowed with a mixed hand may generally be described as "Jack of all trades and master of none." Such people are less exclusive, and more tolerant of all classes and creeds, than those of the pronounced and certain types.

237.
Value of the type.

238.
Character-
istics of the
type.

Such subjects attain to a certain skill in a quantity of pursuits, but seldom attain to an excellence in, or a complete mastery of, any particular one ; they have been well described as handy, interesting men, who, to talk to, are always amusing, but seldom if ever instructive. Their intelligence is large and comprehensive rather than strong in any particular direction ; they can suit themselves instantly to the company in which they find themselves, and can generally make themselves at home in any discussion which may arise.

239.
Advisability
of selection.

The only chance they have of becoming really distinguished, is to take the best talent they have, and cultivate that one to the exclusion of the others ; but they seldom have the strength of purpose to effect this.

240.
Advantages
of the type.

At the same time there are cases where it may be an advantage to possess a mixed hand—as, for instance, where the idealism of a pointed hand is modified and subdued to reason by the fusion of the square hand, such a hand combining imagery *and* reason.

241.
Combination
of the artistic
and element-
ary types.

A common form of mixed hand is that which combines the artistic and the elementary ; and this becomes more comprehensible if you have followed carefully those two types ; for the intelligence of art or music, and the worship of the beautiful, are the only feelings to which the true elementary hand is at all susceptible, and the artistic hand, by the exaggeration of its failings, may often degenerate into the artistic-elementary. Such a hand will betoken a vacillating, unreliable, apathetic character, without sympathy for the misfortunes, or gratification at the good-luck of others. Such people are rude poets, superstitious, and very sensitive to bodily pain. Such hands denote activity by their hardness, and credulity by their pointed tips.

242.
Appearance
and instincts.

Hands of the artistic-elementary type are softer and narrower than those of the purely elementary variety, their fingers are thick and smooth, the thumb gross and conic, the hands closing more easily than they open. Their prevailing instincts are selfishness and greed ; they are not good at manual labor or industry of any sort, but they excel in negotiations and schemes of self-aggrandizement.

A hand half psychic and half elementary will give us innocence and want of capacity for self-protection. Such subjects will be constantly deceived by the unprincipled. They have no head for business, but only a desire for a quiet, passive, Arcadian life, unintellectual and absolutely harmless, *until* a poetic idea of justice shall rouse it, when its bigoted enthusiasm is as sublime as it is deplorable.

243. Elementary and psychic.

A combination of the square and the conic will give us the *finesse* and cunning of the square type, with the demoralization of the conic, and the result will be a great hypocrisy and talent for deception.

244. Square and conic.

If your hand is at the same time square and spatulated, to the energy of the spatulate hand will be added the exactitude, the regularity of the square type. You will have the same love of colossal architecture, but will require it to be regular and arranged. You will have the talents of the tactician, of the strategist, of the diplomatist, and of the constructive scientist. Theory, method, and science will be the mainsprings of your activity.

245. Square and spatulate.

Squareness, confounding itself with spatulation, will give you a love of the minutiæ of an intellectual existence. You will love to do your own menial work for yourself. You will have a wonderful *practical* knowledge, which will incline to a fanaticism of admiration for things which are practical and useful.

246. Square and spatulate.

These fusions are practically without limit, and it is the task of the cheirognomist, which of all others brings out his skill and aptitude in the science of cheirosophy, to decipher and properly to interpret them. Their prevailing character is always [as may be supposed] vivacity, ubiquity, plurality of pursuits and accomplishments, combined with laziness, insincerity, and want of application and perseverance.

247. General characteristics.

5

SUB-SECTION III.

THE CHEIROGNOMY OF THE FEMALE HAND.

248.
Preliminary.

ALL that has been said in the preceding sub-section must [it should be understood] be taken to apply to woman as well as to man; but at the same time the cheirosophist must take into consideration the vast differences of constitution which exist between the sexes, and which, in fact, constitute the base of the relative positions in which they stand to one another.

249.
Difference in the effects of types.

The characteristics of the more powerful types [such as the spatulate and the square] will be much less developed with them than with men, by reason of the greater softness which always characterizes the hands of the "softer sex." In like manner only very few women have knotty hands—a circumstance arising from that absence of physical and mental combination and calculation which, as a rule, characterizes their movements. Thus they work more by tact than by knowledge, more by quickness of brain than by rapidity of action, and more by imagination and intuition than by judgment or combination.

250.
Jointed fingers.

When a woman has knotty fingers, she is less impressionable, less imaginative, less tasteful, less fantastic, and more reasonable.

251.
Effects of the thumb.

If a woman have a large thumb, she is more intelligent than intuitively quick. If she have a small thumb, she is quicker in expedient than intelligent in action. The first will have a taste for history, the second for romance.

With a large thumb, a woman will be sensible and cautious in affairs of the heart. Love is with her a "goodly estate" and not a passion. She will be sagacious, easy of conquest, *or else* unapproachable. There is no medium, for she will never descend to coquetry or jealousy.

If a woman have a small thumb, she will be more capricious, more *coquette*, more prone to jealousy, more fascinating, and more seductive than if she have a large thumb. If the rest of her hand is weak, her character may also be weak, uncertain, irritable, and careless ; now enthusiastic, now despondent and apathetic ; whilst, confiding and naïve, it is impossible for her to keep a secret. With her, love is a passion, an emotion, powerful and fervid. She will demand an undivided fidelity, and a sentimental, romantic form of adoration.

The elementary hand is hardly ever found amongst women. Their natural intelligence, the cares of maternity, the exquisite and complicated physical constitutions of women requiring a higher instinct, a greater intuitive intelligence than is ever constitutionally necessary to man. Consequently, in countries where, amongst the men, the elementary type predominates, the women always have the upper hand, and direct the affairs of their husbands.

Women who live only an objectless, butterfly life of pleasure, love, and luxury, have small conic hands, soft and rather thick.

English women, taking, as they do, so large a part in the administration and arrangement of household affairs, have their fingers for the most part delicately squared.

Women who have an innate curiosity have their fingers so much of different forms and shapes that, when the fingers are closed together and held up against the light, there are chinks and crannies between them through which the light is visible. When, on the other hand, the fingers fit so tightly against one another as to show no light between them when so held up, it is a sign of avarice and meanness, or, at any rate, of want of generosity. And these last two indications apply equally to men [47].

258.
Spatulate fingers and small thumb.

Women with spatulate fingers and a little thumb are warm friends, affectionate and impulsive, unreserved and active, fond of exercise, of animals, and of witnessing feats of skill or strength. Their needlework is useful and complete rather than artistic and showy, and they like to manage and make much of children, whether their own or other people's.

259.
Square fingers and small thumb.

With square fingers and a small thumb we get punctuality, order, and arrangement in household affairs, well regulated and neatly appointed, and a highly developed instinct of real life and of the things which make it tolerable. Square-fingered women require courtesy, order, and regulation in affairs of the heart; they like men to be distinguished without being eccentric, spirited without being wild, quiet, self-confident, and self-contained, untinged by jealousy, or inconstancy; they are particularly careful of social observance. If, however, the squareness is too pronounced, we find a fussy and irritating disposition.

260.
Large thumb.

With a large thumb and square or spatulate fingers we find the tyrannical, "worrying" woman, impatient of control, loud-voiced, and abusive of power when it is intrusted to her.

261.
"Pretty" hands.

A little rosy, soft, smooth hand, thin, but not bony, and with little joints slightly developed, indicates a vivacious, sparkling little woman. To win her you must be bright, clever, witty, spontaneous, amusing; and sparkling, rather than romantic and sentimental, as you must be with the conic-fingered woman.

262.
Conic fingers.

With the latter you must be ardent, timid, self-assured, humble; explaining, excusing, justifying all things. Such women are generally indolent, fantastic, and strongly inclined to sensuality.

With slight, smooth, pointed fingers, a small thumb, and a narrow palm, we find in the subject the highest romanticism and ideality as regards affairs of the world [for which they are eminently unsuited] and of the heart [in which their ideal is never attained]. Pleasure is with them more a matter of heart and soul than of physical emotion. They combine fervor and indolence, and they have the utmost disregard for the conventionalities and realities of life ; they are more prone to excessive piety and superstitious worship than to real devotion. Genius is a thing with them infinitely superior to common sense, and from the height of their radiant idealism they look down upon all intelligences of the beautiful in the abstract which are less sublime than theirs.

263. Small pointed hands.

With the data given above the student of cheirosophy will easily learn to distinguish between the indications of identical formations according as he finds them on the male or on the female hand.

AFTERWARDS.—In the compass of three sub sections, the student has been presented with all such outlines as are necessary for him to learn, of the important first section of the science of cheirosophy. A few moments' reflection will convince him of the vital necessity for mastering this branch of the science of the hand, and of combining it inextricably with the practice of the more profound cheiromancy, to which we are about to turn.

264. Afterwards.

Cheiromancy.

SECTION II.

CHEIROMANCY; OR, THE DEVELOPMENTS AND LINES OF THE PALM.

CHEIROMANCY is that branch of the science of cheirosophy which
reveals not only the habits and temperaments of men, but also the events of their past, the conditions of their present, and the circumstances of their future lives, by the inspection and interpretation of the formations of the palm of the hand, and the lines which are traced thereon. We have seen how necessary it is that in making a cheirognomic examination of a subject the inspection should be conducted with a due regard to the cheiromancy of the hands; it will be seen immediately how much more important it is that the shapes of the hands and fingers should be considered in giving a cheiromantic explanation of any submitted palm. For what is clearer and more easily to be understood than that the character and temperament of a man [chiefly revealed by the cheirognomic examination of his hands] should very greatly influence, even if it does not absolutely bring about, the events which are recorded in his palms, so that a glance at the fingers and thumb will nearly always explain anything which appears doubtful in the palm, and by making a preliminary cheirognomic examination of a subject, the cheiromantic examination will be rendered very much clearer and easier of interpretation. Therefore we combine cheirognomy with cheiromancy far more than cheiromancy with cheirognomy, with a view to rendering this exposition easier of remembrance.

We shall consider in turn the mounts and the lines of the palm, with the signs and other modifications which it is necessary to bear in mind ; but first, we must arrive at a complete understanding of the various parts of the hand, of the lines traced in the palm, and of the names by which they are known to cheirosophists.

266.
Astrologic names of the Mounts.

The names given to the Mounts [those of the principal planets] are not given to them by reason of any astrologic signification which they were at one time supposed to bear, but because we have been accustomed to connect certain characteristics with certain gods of the pagan mythology, and because it is therefore convenient to give to the formations of the hand which reveal certain characteristics the names of the particular gods whose characteristics those were ; a principle obviously more reasonable than to describe geographically in every instance the locality [in the hand] of the formation which it is desired to designate ; therefore it will be understood that in using these astrological terms, such as "The Mount of Venus" or "The Plain of Mars," they are used to indicate the characteristic portrayed by a development of the hand at a certain point.

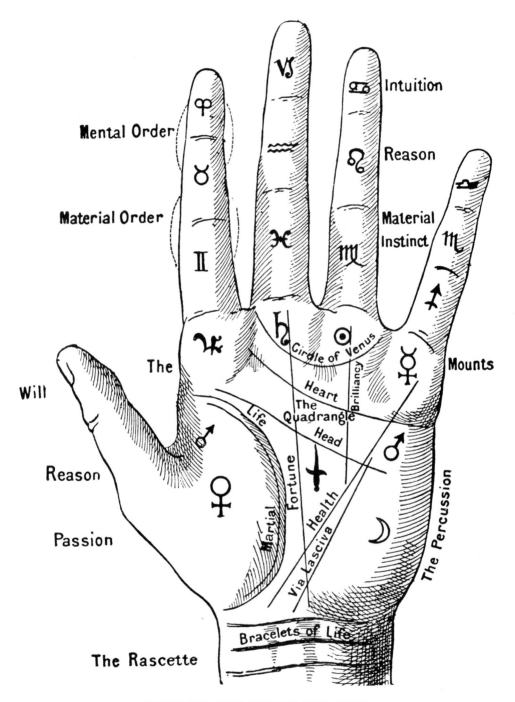

Mental Order

Material Order

The

Will

Reason

Passion

The Rascette

Intuition

Reason

Material
Instinct

Circle of Venus

Brilliancy

Mounts

Heart

The
Quadrangle

Head

Life

Fortune

Martial

Health

Via Lasciva

The Percussion

Bracelets of Life

PLATE VII.—THE MAP OF THE HAND.

SUB-SECTION I.

ON Plate VII. you will find a complete map of the hand, whereon is written the specific and technical name given to each part thereof, the mounts being indicated in their proper position by the planetary signs [♀. ♃. ♄. ☉. ☿. ♂. and ☽.] for the sake of brevity and clearness.

267.
The map of the hand.

The thumb is consecrated to Venus [♀], and at its base will be found the Mount of Venus, surrounded by the Line of Life. The base, or "ball" of the thumb, is frequently looked upon as a phalanx distinct from the hand, but, cheirosophically speaking, the thumb has but two phalanges, the base being termed the Mount of Venus.

268.
The thumb and Mount of Venus.

The first finger [or index] is that of Jupiter [♃], and at its base [*i.e.*, immediately below it, at the top of the palm] will be found the Mount of Jupiter.

269.
First finger Jupiter.

The second finger [or middle finger] is that of Saturn [♄], and the mount which should be found immediately below it is the Mount of Saturn.

270.
Second finger Saturn.

The third finger [or ring finger] is termed the finger of Apollo [☉] [or of the Sun], and the Mount of Apollo will be found, if present, at its base.

271.
Third finger Apollo.

The fourth finger [or little finger] is that of Mercury [☿], whose mount will in like manner be found immediately beneath it.

272.
Fourth finger Mercury.

Just below the Mount of Mercury [between the Line of Heart and the Line of the Head] is the Mount of Mars [♂].

273.
Mount of Mars.

274.
Mount of Moon.

Underneath this last mount, and extending from it to the wrist, is found the Mount of the Moon [☽].

275.
Plain of Mars.

The whole of the centre of the palm is occupied by the Plain or Triangle of Mars, which is comprised between the Line of Life, the Line of Head, and the Mounts of Mars and the Moon.

276.
The Triangle.

This part of the hand is also called the triangle, and is composed of the upper angle—*i.e.*, that formed by the junction of the Lines of Life and of Head ; the inner angle—*i.e.*, that formed by the junction of the Line of Head with the Line of Health or the Line of Fate, at the Mount of the Moon ; and the lower angle, which is formed by the approximation or junction of the Line of Life and the Line of Health [when the latter is present].

277.
The quadrangle.

The quadrangle is the rectangular space comprised between the Lines of Head and of Heart, and is generally bounded on the one side by the Line of Fate and on the other by the Line of Apollo.

278.
The rascette.

The rascette or restreinte is the point on the wrist at which it joins the hand, which is generally occupied by one or more lines, which are more or less apparent, the upper one of which is known as the rascette and the others as the restreintes, the whole forming what are called the Bracelets of Life.

279.
Line of Life.

The lines generally found in the hands are as follows :—The Line of Life, which encircles the ball of the thumb, or Mount of Venus ;

280.
Line of Head.

The Line of Head, which, starting from the beginning of the Line of Life [to which it is usually joined], between the thumb and first finger, runs straight across the hand ;

281.
Line of Heart.

The Line of Heart, which, starting from the Mount of Jupiter or of Saturn, runs across the hand immediately below the Mounts of Saturn, Apollo, and Mercury, ending at the percussion ;

282.
Line of Fortune.

The Line of Fate or Fortune, which, starting either from the Line of Life, from the rascette, or from the Mount of the Moon, runs up more or less directly to the middle finger [the finger of Saturn] ;

The Line of Health or Liver, which, starting near the wrist, at the base of the Line of Life, rises diagonally across the hand to meet the Line of Head, close to the Mount of Mars, or at the top of the Mount of the Moon ; *and*

283. Line of Health.

The Line of Art and Brilliancy, which, rising from the triangle or its vicinity, rises to the finger of Apollo [the third], cutting across the mount at its base.

284. Line of Apollo.

To these are added three lesser lines sometimes found in a hand, which are :—The Line of Mars, which lies close inside the Line of Life, which it follows as a sister line [426 and 444] ;

285. Line of Mars.

The ring or girdle of Venus, which encloses the Mounts of Saturn and of Apollo ; *and*

286. Girdle of Venus.

The Via Lasciva, or milky way, which, rising from the wrist, traverses the Mount of the Moon.

287. Via Lasciva.

The principal lines are also known by other technical names, which [to avoid repetition] will sometimes be used in the following pages. Thus the Line of Life is also called the Vital. The Line of Head is also called the Natural. The Line of Heart is also called the Mensal. The Line of Fortune is also called the Saturnian. The Line of Art, or Brilliancy, is also called the Apollonian, and the Line of Health is often known as the Hepatic.

288. Equivalent names.

The ancient Cheiromants used also to consider the twelve phalanges of the fingers as representing the twelve signs of the Zodiac, and used therefrom to predict the seasons at which certain events would come to pass. This is a branch of cheirosophy which, it is needless to say, is now obsolete, having been refined away with the rest of the dross which used to disguise the pure metal of the science ; but they have been put into the diagram, as they may be interesting to my readers.

289. The signs of the Zodiac.

Having, therefore, mastered what may be called the geography of the hand, we can now turn to the consideration of the cheiro-

290. Cheiro-mancy.

mancy of the hand, commencing with the mounts, and continuing
with the lines; but before entering into the minute discussion
and examination of each particular mount and of each particular
line, I wish to devote a sub-section to the enunciation of certain
general principles, which, applying to all mounts and lines equally,
must be carefully borne in mind throughout every cheiromantic
examination.

291.
Modus
operandi.

The modus operandi of cheirosophy, or the method in which
the Cheirosophist should proceed when he undertakes the examination of a subject, has been relegated to the conclusion of this
work, it being thought advisable to present a thorough knowledge
of the branches of cheirosophy before presenting the principles of
practice.

SUB-SECTION II.

GENERAL PRINCIPLES TO BE BORNE IN MIND.

CHAPTER I.

As to the Mounts.

THE mount which is the highest in the hand will [as we shall see] give the keynote to the character of the subject, and will be the first thing sought for; and when the characteristics are thus pronounced by the development of a particular mount, the lesser [but still noticeable] development of another mount will indicate that the characteristics of the lesser will influence those of the greater, modifying, and in a manner perfecting, those of the reigning development.

292.
The leading mount and the lesser mounts.

You will seldom find that a subject has only one mount developed, and you must bear in mind in all cases that the modifying characteristics must be considered in reading the primary indications of the principal mount.

293.
Modifying indications.

A characteristic betrayed by a prevailing mount can never lie dormant in a subject; opportunities for exercising the qualities indicated will always arise, for the subject will, in a way, make them himself—*e.g.*, a man whose leading mount is that of Mars will, by provoking others, call the talents of his character into play.

294.
Action of a quality.

If a subject have *no* particularly prominent mount in his hand—*i.e.*, all the mounts are equal—you will find a singular regularity of mind and harmony of existence to be his lot.

295.
Equality of the mounts.

If all the mounts are null, and the places where they should be are merely occupied by a plain or a hollow, you will find that the subject has never had any opportunity of developing any particular characteristic, and the life will be a purely negative one.

297.
Other indica-
tions of the
leading
mount.

Excess.

A mount may, instead of being high, be *broad* and full, or it may be covered with little lines. These conditions of the mount give it the same effect as if it were highly developed; and it must be remarked that, if a mount is much covered by lines, it will betray an excess and over-abundance of the qualities of the mount, which prove an insurmountable obstacle to the good effects thereof. Excess of a mount does not give *force*, but *fever* to its quality, producing monomanias, especially if the thumb and Line of Head are weak.

One line upon a mount just emphasizes it enough to be a fortunate sign upon it; *two* lines show uncertainty in the operation of the qualities, especially if they are crossed; and *three*, except in some rare cases, give misfortune arising from the qualities of the mount, *unless* they be even, straight, and parallel. If no other mount is developed, the one upon which most lines are found will be the leading mount in the hand.

Lines placed *crosswise* upon a mount always denote obstacles, and seriously interfere with the goodness of other main lines, which end upon the mount, as in the cases of the mounts and lines of Saturn, or of Apollo, *unless* the ascending line is deeper than the cross lines, in which case the evil indications of the cross lines are destroyed.

De Peruchio affirms that little capillary cross lines upon a mount signify wounds; thus on the Mount of Jupiter they signify a wound to the head; and on that of Saturn, to the breast; on that of Apollo, to the arms; on that of Mercury, to the legs; and on that of Venus, to the body. Some strange confirmations of this statement have been encountered, but such instances are rare.

Thus it will be seen that the indications afforded by any particular mount may be greatly modified, if not annulled, by the appearance of lines upon it, or in its immediate vicinity, so that these must be carefully sought for and examined concomitantly.

It will be very frequently found that the mounts are not exactly under the fingers, but lean, as it were, in the direction of the neighboring mount. In such cases the prevailing development takes a modification from that towards which it inclines.

Finally, the influence of the mount which is principally developed may be either good or bad ; this may be determined by inspecting the formation of the tips of the fingers, the consistency of the hand, and the development of the thumb. Thus, pointed fingers reveal an intuition, a lofty *idealism* of the quality. Square fingers will look at the *reasonable* aspects of character, and spatulate will cultivate the *material* qualities of the mount—*e.g.*, Jupiter developed will indicate, with pointed fingers, religion ; with square fingers, pride ; and with spatulate fingers, tyranny. Apollo developed will indicate, with pointed fingers, love of glory ; with square fingers, realism in art ; and with spatulate fingers, love of wealth and luxury. And so on with the other mounts.

Many writers have gone into the phrenological and physiognomical characteristic of each type, but as this is not only confusing, but irrelevant to the study of pure cheiromancy, the consideration of this matter has been avoided.

6

CHAPTER II.

As to the Lines.

305.
Proper appearance.

THE lines in a hand should be clear and apparent. They should be neat and well colored [not broad and pale], free from branches, breaks, inequalities, or modifications of any sort, except in some few cases, which will be pointed out in due course. A broad pale line always signifies [by indicating excess] a defect of, and obstacle to, the natural indications and qualities of the line.

306.
Pale lines.

Pale lines signify a phlegmatic or lymphatic temperament, with a strong tendency towards effeminacy [women nearly always have very pale lines]. Such subjects are easily put out, and as easily calmed again; they are generally liberal, and subject to strong enthusiasms, which are of short duration.

307.
Red lines.

Red lines indicate a sanguine temperament, and are good; such subjects are gay, pleasant in manner, and honest.

308.
Yellow lines.

Yellow lines denote biliousness and feebleness of the liver; such subjects are quick-tempered, prompt in action, generally ambitious, vigilant, vindictive, and proud.

309.
Livid lines.

Livid lines, with a tendency towards blackishness, betray a melancholy and often a revengeful disposition. Such subjects are grave in demeanor and cunning in character, affable, but haughty; and these indications are the more certain if the fingers are long and the thumb is broad.

310.
Black spots on a line.

Black spots upon a line indicate always nervous diseases, whilst livid holes betray the presence of an organic affection of the part corresponding with the line [Fig. 1, Plate VIII.].

Fig. 1. Spots upon a line

Fig. 2. Sister lines.

Fig. 3. Forked Terminations

Fig. 4. Tasselled Terminations.

a

b

Ascending branches (a)
& Descending branches (b)

Fig. 6. Chained lines.

Fig. 7. Wavy lines.

Fig. 8. Broken lines

Fig. 9. Capillaried lines.

Conditions of the lines.

PLATE VIII.

It must be noted that, however well colored lines may be, a feeble development of the mounts will counteract their good indications.

311. Feeble mounts.

The ancient cheiromants used to affirm that people who had been born in the daytime had the lines clearer marked in the right hand, whilst those who had been born in the night had them more apparent in the left.

312. Persons born by night or by day.

It must also be noted that lines may enlarge, diminish, and even disappear, so that the province of the cheirosophist is [709] to indicate the present condition and indications of the lines, and the likelihood of their future modification. There is one thing to be noted in connection with this matter, which is, that the indications of cunning never alter or become modified; cunning being a characteristic which is acquired, and a characteristic thus acquired is never lost by a weak character on account of inability to free itself, nor by a strong one from a disinclination to do so.

313. Alteration of lines.

Again, in reading the lines a *single* indication must never be accepted as final, especially if it is a bad one. To make *any* indication certain [whether good or bad] corroborating signs must be sought for in both hands, and the absence of corroboration in one hand will contradict, or at any rate greatly modify, any evil sign in the other. A single sign only affords a presumption of the tendency or event which it indicates, and the cause of the danger must be found in the aspect of the mounts, and other lines of the palm, or the development and formations of the whole hand. In the same way, the indication of prudence in the second joint of the thumb will go far towards modifying an evil prognostic which may be found in the palm.

314. Necessity for appearance of indications in *both* hands.

When any principal line is accompanied throughout its course by a second line lying close to it, the principal line is greatly strengthened and benefited by this "sister line," as it is called.

315. Sister lines.

The consecutiveness of the sister will contradict the evils foreshadowed by a break in the principal line [426], but if *both* are broken, the evils are the more certainly to be feared [Fig. 2, Plate VIII.].

316.
Very many lines in the palm

If the hand is covered with a multiplicity, a network of little lines which cross one another in all directions, it betrays a mental agitation and dissatisfaction with one's surroundings, and one's self. It is always the outcome of a highly nervous temperament; and in a soft spatulate hand these little lines denote hypochondria.

317.
Fork at the end of a line.

A fork at the end of a line is often a good sign, for it increases the powers of the lines without carrying them too far. At the same time, it often indicates a duplicity in connection with the qualities of the line [484] [Fig. 3].

318.
Tasselled at end.

When the fork is reduplicated so as to form a tassel at the end of the line, the indication is bad, denoting feebleness and nervous palpitation of the organ represented [Fig. 4].

319.
Ascending and descending branches.

All branches *rising* from a line increase its good indications, whereas all *descending* branches accentuate its bad qualities. Ascending branches indicate richness, abundance of the qualities appertaining to a line ; thus on the Line of Heart they denote warmth of affection and devotion ; on the Line of Head they denote cleverness and intelligence ; on the Line of Saturn they denote good luck, and so on. These branches, when present, are nearly always found at the beginnings and endings of lines [Fig. 5].

320.
Chained lines.

A chained formation of a line indicates obstacles, struggles, and contrarieties of the characteristics afforded by it [Fig. 6].

321.
Wavy lines.

A wavy formation [Fig. 7] of a line signifies ill-luck, as does also a break in it. Breaks may be either simple interruptions or cessations of the line, or bars across it : They are always a bad sign, and the interrupting influence must be carefully sought [Fig. 8].

Fig. 10.
The Star

Fig. 11.
The Square

Fig. 12.
The Spot

Fig. 13.
The Circle

Fig. 14.
The Island

Fig. 15.
The Triangle

Fig. 16.
The Cross

Fig. 17.
The Grille

Signs found in the Hand.

PLATE IX.

When a line, instead of being single and clear, is composed of a number of little capillaries, which here and there, or at the ends, unite to form a single line, it betrays obstacles and ill-success, in the same way as chained lines [Plate VIII., Fig. 9].

322.
Capillaries.

SUB-SECTION III.

THE MOUNTS OF THE HANDS.

323.
The prevailing mount.

The prevailing mount is the first thing to be observed in the palm of a hand, and it must be sought for with a careful regard to the general principles laid down in Sub-section II. In this sub-section we shall carefully consider the indications afforded by each mount in succession, as well as those of some of the principal combinations of mounts.

CHAPTER I.

The Mount of Jupiter [♃].

THE predominance of this mount in a hand denotes a genuine and reverential feeling of religion, a worthy and high ambition, honor, gayety, and a love of nature. It also denotes a love of display, of ceremony, and of pomp, and is, consequently, generally developed in the hands of public entertainers of any sort. Such subjects talk loudly, are extremely self-confident, are just and well-minded, gallant and extravagant, and are always impetuous without being revengeful. These subjects are fond of flattery and fond of good living. They generally marry early, and are always well-built and handsome, having a certain *hauteur*, which enhances their charms without detracting from their good nature.

324.
Indications of the mount.

An excessive development of the mount will give arrogance, tyranny, ostentation, and, with pointed fingers, superstition. Such subjects will be votaries of pleasure, and vindictive, sparing nothing to attain their selfish ends.

325.
Excess of the mount.

If the mount is absent [*i.e.*, replaced by a cavity] the subject is prone to idleness and egoism, irreligious feelings, want of dignity, and a license which degenerates into vulgarity.

326.
Absence of the mount.

The development of this mount gives to square fingers a great love of regularity and established authority. To long smooth fingers it imparts a love of luxury, especially if the fingers are large at the third phalanx [41]. This mount *ought* always to be accompanied by a smooth, elastic, firm hand [not too hard], with a well-developed first phalanx to the thumb [Will].

327.
With square and smooth fingers.

328.
Influence of Saturn.

If to the good indications of this mount a favorably developed finger, or Mount of Saturn, be added, the success in life and good fortune of the subject is certain; Saturn denoting fatality, whether for good or evil.

329.
Lines on the mount.

A single line upon the mount indicates success. Many and confused lines upon the mount betray a constant, unsuccessful struggle for greatness, and if these confused lines are crossed, they denote unchastity, no matter which the sex of the subject.

330.
Cross and star on the mount.

A cross upon the mount denotes a happy marriage, and if a star be found there as well as the cross, it indicates a brilliant and advantageous alliance.

331.
Spot.

A spot upon the mount indicates a fall of position, and loss of honor or credit.

332.
Its religion.

A long thumb and a development of the first joint in the fingers will give to this mount free thought and irreverence in religion. If, besides these, we find pointed fingers and what is called the "Croix Mystique," you will find ecstasy in matters religious, tending even to fanaticism.

333.
Displacement of the mount.

If, instead of being in position immediately underneath the finger of Jupiter [or forefinger], the mount is displaced and inclines towards that of Saturn, it acquires a serious tone and demeanor, and gives a desire for success in science, theology, or classical scholarship.

334.
Combinations of the mount with others.

If with the Mount of Jupiter we find also the Mount of Apollo [☉] developed, it indicates good fortune and wealth. Combined with the Mount of Mercury [☿], we find a love of exact science and philosophy. Such subjects are inclined to be poetic, are well behaved and clever; they make the most successful doctors. To a bad hand this combination will give vanity, egoism, a love of chatter, fanaticism, charlatanry, and immorality. Combined with the Mount

Mars.

of Mars [♂] it gives audacity and the talent of strategy. Such subjects are self-confident, successful, and fond of celebrity. To a bad hand such a combination gives insolence, ferocity, revolt, dissipation, and inconstancy. A combination of the Mounts of Jupiter and Moon. of the Moon [☽] makes a subject honorable, placid, and just. With Venus. the Mount of Venus [♀] a subject of this Jupiterian type becomes sociable, simple-minded, gay, sincere, fond of pleasure, and generous. If the hand is, on the whole, bad, the combination will denote effeminacy, feeble-mindedness, caprice, and a love of debauch.

CHAPTER II.

The Mount of Saturn [♄].

335.
Effects of
the mount.

THE predominance of this mount in a hand denotes a character in which to prudence and natural caution is added a *fatality** for good or evil, which is extreme. Such subjects are always sensitive and particular about little things, even though their fingers be short [26–27]. The mount also denotes a tendency to occult science, to incredulity, and to epicureanism of temperament. Such subjects are always inclined to be morbid and melancholy. They are timid, and love solitude, and a quiet life in which there is neither great good fortune nor great ill fortune ; they are also fonder of serious music than of gay melody. They take naturally to such pursuits as agriculture, horticulture, or mineralogy, having a natural *penchant* for anything connected with the earth. These subjects seldom marry, are extremely self-centred and self-confident, and care nothing for what other people may think of them.

336.
Excessive de-
velopment of
the mount.

The mount is seldom *very* high, for fatality is always, to a certain extent, modifiable ; but when there is an excess of formation on this mount it betrays taciturnity, sadness, an increased morbidity and love of solitude, remorse and asceticism, with the horrible opposing characteristics of an intense fear and horror of death, with a morbid tendency to, and curiosity concerning suicide. The evil indications of an excessive development may be greatly modified by a well-formed Mount of Venus [♀].

* By fatality is meant *certainty*, *i.e.*, the indications of the middle finger are always looked upon as certain and unavoidable.

The Saturnian hand has generally long, bony fingers, which give it philosophy, the second finger [that of Saturn] is large, with the first [or nailed] phalanx highly developed, the mount, if not high, being generally strongly lined. A bad Saturnian hand has a hard, rough skin and a thick wrist.

337.
"Saturnian"
hand.

If the mount is quite absent the indication is of an insignificant, "vegetable" existence, unmoved by any great depth of feeling, and one which is continually oppressed by a sense of misfortune. But when it is thus absent it may be replaced by a well-traced Line of Fate [or Saturn].

338.
Absence of
the mount.

A single straight line upon the mount signifies good fortune and success, whilst a plurality of lines thereon indicates a proportionate ill-luck. A succession of little lines placed ladder-wise across the mount and extending upon that of Jupiter indicates an easy and gradual progression to high honor.

339.
Lines on the
mount.

A spot upon the mount always indicates an evil fatality, the cause of which must be sought for upon the Lines of Head or of Fate.

340.
Spot on the
mount.

If a branch [not the end of the Line of Heart or of Saturn] rises from the Line of Heart on to the Mount of Saturn, it denotes worry, travail, and anxiety ; if the branch is clean and single, however, it will foreshadow wealth as a result of those anxieties [*l*, in Plate X.].

341.
Branch from
the Line of
Heart.

If, instead of being in its proper position beneath the second finger, the mount is displaced towards Jupiter, it has the same significance as the displacement of the Mount of Jupiter towards Saturn [333]. If, on the other hand, it is displaced towards the Mount of Apollo, it betokens a fatality which can be, and must be, striven against.

342.
Displace-
ment of the
mount.

If, together with the Mount of Saturn, we find the Mount of Jupiter developed, we shall find gentleness, patience, and respect in a good hand, or want of appreciation, inability to make use of

343.
Combination
with other
mounts.

opportunities, melancholy, hysteria, and want of taste in a bad hand. Combined with that of Mercury this mount gives us antiquarian research, and love of science from an "amateur" point of view, a talent for medicine, and a desire for information on various subjects. Such subjects are clever at individualizing and classing, and are generally happy. And this latter indication generally holds good even when the rest of the hand is bad, in which case the combination of Saturn and Mercury gives us perfidy, perjury, sullen temper, revenge, theft, want of filial affection, and charlatanry.

344.
Further combinations.
Mars.

Venus.

Moon.

With the Mount of Mars equally developed this mount betokens aggressiveness, bitterness of humor, a false superiority, insolence, immodesty, and cynicism. The combination of the Mounts of Venus and Saturn will give us a love of and a search after truth in matters occult, piety, charity, logic, self-control, with a tendency to jealousy and love of display. If the hand is bad the combination will betray frivolity, curiosity, and, if the Mount of Saturn be the more strongly developed of the two, we shall find pride, envy, and debauchery. When the Mounts of the Moon and of Saturn find themselves equally developed in a hand, we have a subject whose intuition and pure talent for occultism is remarkably developed. It is a curious fact that these latter subjects are generally frightfully ugly.

CHAPTER III.

The Mount of Apollo [☉].

A HAND in which this mount is developed is essentially that of a subject whose prevailing tastes and instincts are artistic, and it always gives to its possessor a greater or a less degree of success, glory, celebrity, and brilliancy of fortune, denoting, as it does, genius, intelligence, tolerance, and wealth, the characteristics of the type being self-confidence, beauty, grace, and tolerance in all things.

345.
Fortune of the mount.

Such subjects are inventive and imitative, being often great discoverers. Their principal failings are, *quick* temper [though not of long duration] and a certain incapacity for very *close* friendships, though they are generally benevolent and generous, even devoted, were it not for the inseparable strain of fickleness. Proud, and eloquent on matters of art, they love anything which is brilliant, such as jewelry and the more ornamental forms of worship, for they are religious from a gratitude for blessings received rather than from a superstitious reverence. They make stern and unrelenting judges, and their love is more affectionate than sensual.

346.
Indications of the mount.

These Apollonian subjects love to shine before the world, and not to be the cynosure of a small circle of admirers, though they hate the idea of ostentation or undeserved glory ; they will not explain themselves in dogmatizing unless they think their audiences are sympathetic, refusing to waste words on ignorant cavillers, or to persuade people to accept their opinions. In marriage they are, un-

347.
Further indications.

fortunately, very often unlucky, for their ideal, their standard of excellence, is unreasonably high.

348.
"Apollonian" hand.
The normal development of a hand bearing this mount high shows smooth fingers, with the tips mixed or slightly squared, the palm of an equal length with the fingers, a well-marked phalanx of logic, and either one very deep, or three strong lines upon the mount.

349.
Excess of the mount.
If the mount is developed to excess it indicates a love of wealth and of extravagance in expenditure, instincts of luxury, fatuity, envy, and curiosity, a quick, unreasoning temper, and a strong tendency to levity, frivolity, and sophistry. Such subjects are boastful, vain, think themselves unappreciated, but highly superior to their fellow-men. This excessive development is generally accompanied, and is emphasized by, twisted fingers, spatulated soft hands, a grille [596] on the mount, with a long phalanx of will and proportionately short phalanx of logic.

350.
Absence of the mount.
If, on the other hand, this mount is absent in both hands, its absence betrays materiality and indifference to matters artistic, giving a dull, unenlightened life.

351.
Lines of the mount.
A single line deeply traced upon the mount indicates fortune and glory; two lines indicate considerable talent, but a great probability of failure, whilst many confused lines show a tendency to lean to the scientific aspects of art.

352.
Development.
If the mount is merely *developed*, having no line marked upon it, it shows a love of the beautiful, but not necessarily a talent for production of works of art.

353.
Spot on the mount.
A spot upon the mount denotes a grave danger of a loss of reputation or caste.

354.
Combination with other mounts. Mercury.
When in a hand the Mounts of Apollo and of Mercury are found equally developed, we find a character in which justice, firmness, perspicacity, love of scientific research, combined with clearness of

diction and eloquence, are salient features. The combination of Apollo and the Moon gives good sense, imagination, reflection, and Moon. light-heartedness. With an equal development of the Mount of Venus, we get amiability and a great desire to please. Venus.

CHAPTER IV.

The Mount of Mercury [☿].

355.
Indications of the mount.
THE preëminence in a hand of this mount indicates science, intelligence, spirit, eloquence, a capacity for commerce, speculation, industry and invention, agility, promptitude in thought and action, and a *penchant* for travel and occult science.

356.
Eloquence.
[The eloquence which is one of the prevailing characteristics of the type is of a kind denoted by the formation of the fingers. A high Mount of Mercury will give, with pointed fingers, brilliant oratory; with square fingers, clearness and reason in expounding; with spatulate fingers, force and vehemence in argument and dogma; with long fingers, details and parentheses; and with short fingers, brevity and conciseness. The great difference between the eloquence of these subjects, and of those whose prevailing mount is that of Apollo, is that the oratory of the former is sophistical and clever, rather than naïve and direct like that of the latter; it is this that makes them such good barristers. To assist their faculties in this respect still further, these subjects should always have short nails (146)].

357.
Further indications.
Such subjects are good athletes, are agile, clever at games of skill, spontaneous in expedients, sharp in practice, with a great capacity for serious studies. Combined with these qualities we generally recognize envy, but amiability therewith; often [the other conditions of the hand being favorable] we find that these subjects are clever clairvoyants, seldom sensual, and generally good-humored, and fond of playing with children so long as they are not otherwise seriously

employed. This tendency to envy, by raising envious feeling at the aptitudes and successes of others, constantly drives these Mercurial subjects to take up and try a great variety of pursuits.

These subjects are great matchmakers, and frequently marry very young, choosing equally young persons for their helpmates.

358. Marriage.

The normal development of the hand which accompanies this mount is as follows : Long, smooth fingers, hard, slightly spatulated [athletics], or very soft with mixed tips [thought] ; the finger of Mercury long and sometimes pointed ; the high mount cut by a deep line, and the philosophic joint developed.

359. Normal development of the type.

If the mount is developed to excess in a hand, it denotes theft, cunning, deceit, treachery, with pretentious ignorance. Such subjects are charlatans, running after the false and dishonest forms of occultism, and are generally superstitious. These hands usually have long twisted fingers, more or less turned back ; soft hands, confused markings on the mount, and the phalanx of will long.

360. Excess.

A complete absence of the mount denotes inaptitude for science or for commercial enterprise.

361. Absence.

A single line upon the mount indicates modesty and moderation, and in many instances a strange, unexpected stroke of good fortune. A cross line extending upon the Mount of Apollo betrays charlatanry in science, and, in fact, the dishonest occultism alluded to above [360]. If this line have an "island" [573] in it and cut the Line of Apollo or Brilliancy, it denotes ill-luck, probably resulting from some perfectly innocent act.

362. Lines on the mount.

Many mixed lines upon the mount denote astuteness and aptitude for sciences. If they reach as low as the Line of Heart, they denote liberality ; and if to numerous rays on this mount a subject join a high Mount of the Moon, his *penchant* for medical science will take the form of hypochondria. The elder cheiromants have affirmed

363. Rayed mount.

7

that a woman having this mount well rayed is sure to marry a doctor, or, at any rate, a man of science. If the lines on the mount merely take the form of little flecks and dashes, it is a practically sure indication of a babbling, chattering disposition.

364.
Lines on the side of the hand.

Lines on the percussion—*i.e.*, on the edge of the hand, between the base of the little finger and the line of heart—indicate *liaisons*, or serious affairs of the heart if horizontal [*i.e.*, parallel with the line of the heart], each line denoting a separate *liaison* or love affair, a single deep line denoting one strong and lasting affection. If vertical they denote, almost invariably, the number of children which the subject has had. *De Peruchio* lays down the rule that if they are strong they denote boys, if faint girls; and if they are short or indistinct the children are either dead or not yet born. Several vertical lines on the percussion, crossed by a line which starts from a star upon the mount, betray sterility, whilst a marriage line, ending abruptly by a star, indicates a marriage or *liaison* of short duration, terminated by death.

365.
Smooth mount.
Grille.
Circle.
Spot.

The mount quite smooth and unlined indicates a cool, determined, and constant condition of mind. A grille upon the mount is a dangerous prognostic of a violent death, a circle also placed upon the mount indicating that it will be by water. A spot upon the mount indicates an error or misfortune in business.

366.
Effect of Apollo.

If the mount is high, and the hand contains a long line of Apollo, the commercial instinct will work itself out in speculation rather than in recognized and persevering commerce.

367.
Displacement of the mount

The mount leaning, as it were, towards that of Apollo is a good sign, good enough to counteract a bad Line of Saturn, betokening science and eloquence. Leaning in a contrary direction [*i.e.*, towards the percussion] it indicates commerce and industry.

368.
Connected with ♀

Connected with the Mount of Venus by a good line, [*ee*, in Plate X.], this mount gives happiness and good fortune.

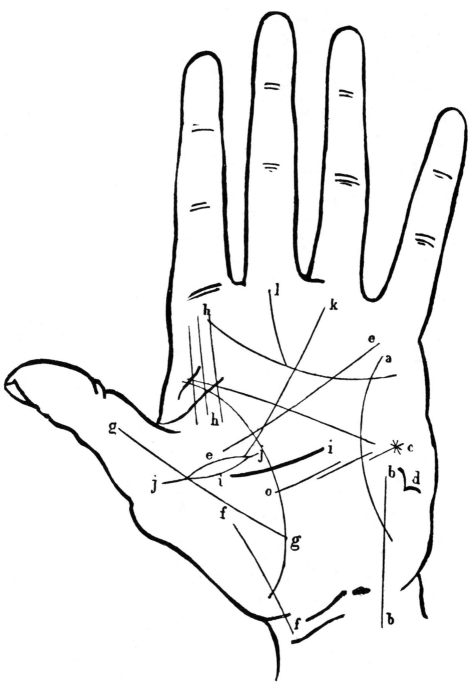

PLATE X.—LINES UPON THE MOUNTS OF THE PALM.

Combined [*i.e.*, equally developed] with the Mount of Venus, we find wit, humor, gayety, love of beauty, often piety, easy and sympathetic eloquence. In a bad hand [*i.e.*, if the fingers are twisted, the Line of Head weak, and the phalanx of will small] this combination will give inconsequence, contradiction, meddlesomeness, inconstancy, and want of perseverance. The combination of Mercury and Saturn in a hand is always good, giving to the sobriety and fatality of Saturn a certain intuitive practicality which seldom fails to give good results. The Mount of Mercury is, however, one which is not often combined with the other mounts of the hand.

369.
Combination
with other
mounts.
Venus.

Saturn.

CHAPTER V.

The Mount of Mars [♂].

370.
Construction
of the Mount
and Plain
of ♂.

THE discussion of the Mount of Mars is not fraught with that simplicity which characterizes that of the other mounts. It is, in a manner, divided into the Mount of Mars, properly so called, which is situated, as may be seen, beneath the Mount of Mercury, on the percussion of the hand; and that development or extension of the mount into the palm of the hand [shown in Plate VII. by a dagger] which is known as the Plain of Mars. It will be seen that a development of the *Mount* of Mars becomes the *Plain* of Mars, by the swelling it produces in that part of the palm occupied by the Triangle [275-6]; and as the Plain of Mars is treated of in the remarks upon the Triangle, but little notice need be taken of it here. The keynote of the whole question may be struck by bearing in mind that the

Interpretation.

Mount of Mars denotes *resistance*, whereas the *Plain* of Mars betrays action and aggression. This will be more fully demonstrated later on.

371.
Characteristics of the
mount.

The main characteristics indicated by a development of the Mount of Mars are courage, calmness, *sangfroid* in moments of emergency, resignation in misfortune, pride, resolution, resistance, and devotion, with a strong capacity to command.

372.
Its indications.

Well developed and not covered by lines or rays, this mount will counteract the evil influences of a short thumb by the calmness and resignation which it imparts to a character. Such a subject [especially if his thumb be large] possesses, to a marked extent, the capacity for keeping his temper. He will be magnanimous and generous to extravagance, loud of voice, and hot-blooded ; his passions carrying him even to sensuality, unless counteracted by a strong phalanx of logic. His eloquence, if he possess that faculty, rare among subjects of this type, will be of the fascinating rather than the emotional description. Spatulate fingers will give to this mount a love of show and self-glory.

These subjects have always a great natural inclination to love, though they nearly always marry late in life, and marry women of the type of Venus [402–3]. These two types seem to have a natural inclination for one another.

373. Marriage, ♂ — ♀.

The hand to which these Martial mounts belong are generally hard, the fingers large, especially at the third phalanx, the will long, and the logic small, the hollow of the hand [Plain of Mars] rayed and lined.

374. Aspect of the hand.

An excessive development of this mount [*i.e.*, a spreading of the mount into the palm, "the Plain of Mars"], or a mass of lines upon the mount, will indicate *brusquerie*, fury, injustice of mind, insolence, violence, cruelty, blood-thirstiness, insult, and defiance of manner. Lines on the mount always denote hot temper. This excessive development generally betrays lasciviousness, and exaggeration in speech.

375. Excess and lines on the mount.

The Plain of Mars highly developed or covered with lines indicates a love of contest, struggle, and war, especially if the nails be short [146] and a cross [586] be found in the plain. This network of little lines in the Plain of Mars always indicates obstacles in the way of real good fortune.

376. Lines on the mount.

These hands of the excessive type have generally a feeble Line of Heart often joined to the Line of Head, the Line of Life red in color, and the thumb short and clubbed.

377. Excessive type of ♂.

If the mount be completely absent, its absence denotes cowardliness and childishness.

378. Absence.

379.
Tradition.

De Peruchio and Taisnier both assert that a line extending from the Mount of Mars to between the Mounts of Jupiter and Saturn, with little spots of the Line of Head, indicates deafness.

380.
Combinations with other mounts.
Apollo.
Moon.

Venus.

Mercury.

Saturn.

Combined with the Mount of Apollo, this mount becomes an indication of ardor and energy in art, force, perseverance, and truth in action. With the Mount of the Moon, we get a love of navigation, or, if the rest of the hand is bad [303], folly. Combined with the Mount of Venus, we find a love of music and of dancing, sensuality, ardor, and jealousy in love. The combination of Mars and Mercury denotes movement and quickness of thought and speech, spontaneity, incredulity, and a love of argument, strife of words, and mockery. An equal development of the Mounts of Saturn and Mars gives cynicism, audacity of belief and opinion, and want of moral sense; we find, in fact, in this case, the energy of Mars rousing to action the usually latent evil qualities of Saturn.

CHAPTER VI.

The Mount of the Moon [☽].

THE attributes of this mount, when found predominant in a hand, are imagination, melancholy, chastity, poetry of soul, and a love of mystery, solitude, and silence, with a tendency to reverie and imagination. To it belongs also the domain of harmony in music, as opposed to the melody, which is the special attribute [as we shall see] of the Mount of Venus.

381.
Its attributes.

Such subjects are generally capricious and changeable, egoists, and inclined to be idle ; their imagination often makes them hypochondriacal, and their abstraction often causes them to develop the faculty of presentiment, giving them intuition, prophetic instincts, and dreams. They are fond of voyages by reason of their restlessness, they are more mystic than religious, phlegmatic in habit, fantastic, and given to romance in matters of art and literature. They make generally the best rhymists, but they have no self-confidence, no perseverance, and no powers of expression in speech. They are much given to capricious marriages, which astonish their friends, from disparity of years, or something of the kind.

382.
Characteristics.

These hands are generally swollen and soft, with short, smooth, and pointed fingers, and a short phalanx of logic. For the influence of the mount to be altogether good, it should be fuller at the base [near the wrist] than at the top [near the Mount of Mars] or in the centre. Excessive fulness in the exact centre generally betrays some internal or intestinal weakness, whilst excessive fulness at the top indicates, as a rule, biliousness, goutiness, and a susceptibility

383.
Formation of the "lunar" hand.

to catarrh. Bad concomitant signs are a forking of the head line [156], a low Mount of Mars, with the Mount of Apollo covered with a grille; then we find betrayed the vices of slander, debauchery, immodesty, insolence, and cowardice.

384.
Hard hand.
The mount developed with a hard hand often betokens a dangerous activity and exercise of the imagination; with spatulate fingers this subject will be constantly forming projects and plans.

385.
Effect of finger tips.
It may well be understood that a development of this mount emphasizes and harmonizes admirably with pointed fingers, but its development makes a square-fingered subject miserable by the constant turmoil and struggle between the realms of fact and fancy, *unless* there appear in the hand a good and well-traced line of Apollo, which will give an artistic turn and instinct to the regularity of the square fingers. But if the fingers of the hand which bears this mount be very long, or *very* square, the inevitable result will be a perpetual discontent.

386.
Suitable fingers.
A development of this hand should always [26–7] be accompanied by short fingers, otherwise the detail indicated by the fingers will be constantly fretting the *laissez aller* instincts of the mount, or the morbid imagination of the mount will turn the detail of the fingers into a positive disease.

387.
Excessive development.
An excessive development of the Mount of the Moon will produce in a character unregulated caprice, wild imaginations, irritability, discontent, sadness, superstition, fanaticism, and error. Such subjects are intensely liable to suffer from headaches; and they take a morbid pleasure in painful thoughts and humiliating reflections.

388.
Long mount.
When the mount is not high, but very long, coming down to the base of the hand, and forming an angle with the wrist, it denotes a resigned and contemplative character, quite devoid of all strength, strength being shown by *thickness*, as opposed to weakness, which is indicated by *length* of the mount.

If the mount is absolutely absent, it betrays want of ideas and imagination, want of poetry of mind, and general drought of the intellect.

389.
Absence.

Highly developed with the " Croix Mystique," well traced in the hand, and pointed fingers, we find *invariably* a wonderful faculty of clairvoyance, which may be marvellously developed and cultivated.

390.
Clairvoyance.

The idleness [382] betrayed in a character by the development of this mount must not be confused with the idleness indicated by softness of the hands [98*a*], the latter denoting idleness of the body, and slothfulness, as opposed to the idleness indicated by the former, which is that of the mind [reflection, etc.].

391.
Idleness.

It sometimes occurs that there is a difficulty in determining the exact boundaries of the Mount of the Moon. It may generally be assumed that it joins the Mount of Mars at the extremity of the Line of the Head, and is separated from the Triangle and the Plain of Mars by either the Line of Saturn, or of Health, or by the Via Lasciva [which is rarely found in a hand, 535].

392.
Boundaries of the mount.

One line upon the mount betrays a vivid instinct, a curious vague presentiment of evils; many lines and rays on the mount denote visions, presentiments, prophetic dreams, and the like. Such subjects are much prone to folly and inconstancy. A single deep ray across the mount, with a small line crossing it, denotes gout or a gouty tendency.

393.
Lines on the mount.

A subject in whose hand is found a clear, strong line from the Rascette to the middle of the mount [as at *bb*, in Plate X.] will be a complaining, fretful person.

394.
Line from the wrist.

A line extending in an arc from the Mount of Mercury to the Mount of the Moon [as at *aa*, in Plate X.], with more or less developed rays upon the mount, is an invariably sure sign of presentiments, prophetic instincts, and dreams.

395.
Connected with ☽ by curved line.

396.
Horizontal
lines.
Voyages.

Horizontal lines traced upon the percussion at the side of the Mount of the Moon denote voyages. Such a travel line terminating with, or interrupted by, a star, indicates that the voyage will be a dangerous, if not a fatal one. If a travel line is so prolonged over the Mount of the Moon into the hand as to cut the Line of Head, making there a star, the subject will suddenly abandon his position and prospects in life, for the sake of a perilous voyage [668].

397.
Star on the
mount.

A star upon the mount, connected by a small line with the Line of Life, is a prognostication of hysteria and madness [*cc*, in Plate X.] when it is accompanied by the other signs of dementia in a hand [478].

398.
Connected
with ☿ by
straight line.

A straight line from the Mount of Mercury to that of the Moon betokens good fortune, arising from the imagination and guiding instinct developed in the mount.

399.
Much cross-
barred.

The mount much cross-barred indicates a condition of constant self-torment and worry, the cause of which will be shown by some strong development elsewhere in the hand, as, for instance, by a development of the Line of Heart [448], which shows that the self-torment is from too much affection; or by a raying of the Mount of Jupiter, which shows ambition to be the disturbing element; or by a like condition of the Mount of Mercury, which indicates that the worries arise from business or commerce. This worrying tendency may, however, be counteracted by very square fingers, or a long phalanx of logic; or it may be annulled by the resistance and resignation of a high Mount of Mars.

400.
Angle or
crescent.

An angle on the mount [*d*, in Plate X.] indicates a great danger of drowning. A crescent in the same place is said to betoken the fatal influence of woman upon one's life. I have not come across these signs in practice.

If in a hand the Mounts of Moon and Mercury are equally devel- **401.**
oped, it is a sign of subtility, changeability, and intuition in the Combinations with
deeper sciences, bringing, as their consequence, success and even other mounts
Mercury.
celebrity. A like combination of the mount with that of Venus results in devotion of a romantic and fantastic kind, curiosity and Venus.
recherché in affairs of the heart. In a bad hand such a combination will give caprice, eccentricity, and unnatural instincts in affairs
of the heart. A combination with Saturn will give hypochondria Saturn.
and cowardice, egotism, slovenliness, and a tendency to indigestion.
The constant attribute of the mount is imagination and fancy.

CHAPTER VII.

The Mount of Venus [♀].

402.
Its characteristics.

THE main attributes of this mount, shown in a character by its prominence in the hand, are the possession of, and an admiration for, beauty, grace, melody in music, dancing, gallantry, tenderness, and benevolence, with a constant desire to please and to be appreciated. It is essentially the Mount of Melody [381], and is, consequently, always to be found in the hands of those who are talented as singers. The attributes of this mount are the more feminine forms of beauty, as contrasted with the masculine forms of beauty, which are indicated by a prominence of the Mount of Jupiter.

403.
Its indications.

These subjects are great lovers of pleasure and society; they are fond of applause, but more from their love of giving pleasure to others than for its own sake. They hate any form of quarrel or strife, and are essentially gay, though they are less noisily gay, as a rule, than subjects of the type of Jupiter. Men of the type are often effeminate; all of them, however, have the talents of painting, poetry, and music, whether they have the perseverance to cultivate them or not.

404.
Modifying effects of ♀.

A development of this mount will always mitigate and soften the harsh effects, or malignities, of any other mount.

405.
The typical hand.

The hands which usually accompany a development of this mount are fat and dimpled, the fingers smooth and rather short, the thumb also short. The *bad* influence of the type is betrayed by extreme softness, pointed fingers, the mount much cross-barred, the

Line of Mars indicated inside the Line of Life, and the Via Lasciva traced upon the palm.

**406.
Excess.**
An excess of the mount will betray debauchery, effrontery, license, inconstancy, vanity, flirtation, and levity.

**407.
Absence.**
The absence of the mount betrays coldness, laziness, and dulness in matters of art. Without this mount developed to a certain extent, all the other passions become dry and selfish in their action.

**408.
Very smooth.**
If the mount is completely devoid of lines, it indicates coldness, chastity, and, very often, a short life.

**409.
Lines on the mount.**
A quantity of lines on the mount denotes always heat of passion and warmth of temperament. If there are but two or three strong lines traced upon the mount, they indicate ingratitude.

**410.
Debauchery.**
A worn-out libertine has always this mount flat, but very much rayed, the Girdle of Venus being also traced in the hand, which indicates that, the desire of the subject being beyond his powers, he constantly seeks for change and new excitement.

**411.
Connected with ☿**
A line extending from the mount to that of Mercury [*ee*, in Plate X.] is always a good sign, indicating good fortune and love resulting from one another.

**412.
Line from wrist.**
A line rising from the base of the hand into the mount is also a sign of good-luck [*ff*, in Plate X.].

**413.
Marriage lines.**
Lines from the phalanx of logic to the Line of Life [*gg*, in Plate X.] are said by many authorities to indicate marriages; and if they are confused, they betray troubles and worries in love and marriage [428].

**414.
Islands.**
Islands [574] placed crosswise upon the mount [*jj*, in Plate X.] indicate advantageous opportunities of marriage which have been missed. These lost opportunities would have been all the more brilliant and desirable if the islands are connected with the Mount of Apollo [as at *k*, in Plate X.] by a line.

415.
Other lines.

Three lines extending straight to the Mount of Jupiter denote liberality and happiness [*hh*, in Plate X.]. A deep line cutting into the triangle [*ii*, in Plate X.] betrays a tendency to asthma.

416.
The seven
types.

It has been an almost invariable rule among cheirosophists to make these mounts the bases and distinguishing characteristics of seven clearly defined types, assigning to each a special physiognomy, phrenology, etc. This, however, is not considered expedient, for the hands have already been divided into seven far more practical and ordinary types [159], and it is but rarely that a hand will be found dominated by one single preëminent mount.

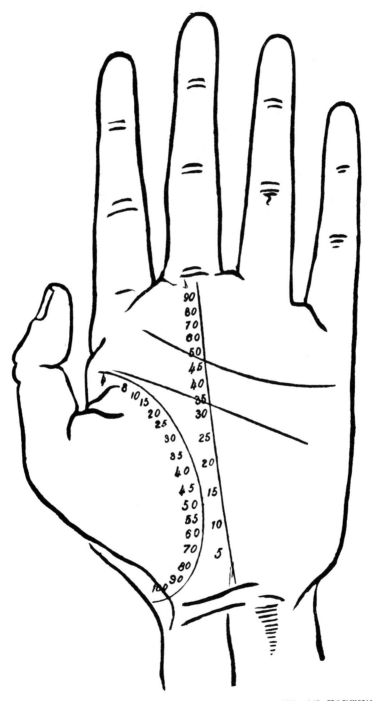

PLATE XI.—AGES UPON THE LINES OF LIFE AND OF FORTUNE.

SUB-SECTION IV.

THE LINES IN THE HAND.

WE shall now consider and discuss each line in turn, according to its relative importance. The great difficulty about the consideration of the lines, in the acquement of the dogma of cheirosophy, is that the amount of details to be learnt by heart is apparently enormous. It is not, however, the case, as will be found when we reach the end of this sub-section, for, as a matter of fact, a complete knowledge of cheiromancy depends merely on a complete comprehension of the indications of the three principal Lines—Head, Heart, and Life. It is the aspect and *condition* of these lines, and the methods and causes of their disarrangments and subdivisions, which, properly observed, afford us all the information we can possibly require.

417.
Simplicity of the study.

CHAPTER I.

The Line of Life.

418.
Proper conditions.

THIS line should be long, completely encircling the ball of the thumb [Mount of Venus], strong, not too broad or too fine, without curvature, breakage, cross bars, or irregularities of any description. Thus marked in a hand, it notes long life, good health, a good character and disposition.

419.
Evil aspects of the line.

Pale and broad, it indicates ill-health, bad instincts, and a feeble and envious character. Thick and red, it betrays violence and brutality of mind; chained [Fig. 6, Plate VIII.], it indicates delicacy of constitution; thin and meagre in the centre, it indicates ill-health during a portion of the life; a spot terminating this thinness indicates sudden death. If it is of various thicknesses throughout its course, it denotes a capricious and fickle temper.

420.
Age on the line.

Perhaps the most important consideration connected with this line is the determination of age. The line is divided up into periods of five and ten years, in the manner shown in Plate XI., and according as irregularities or breaks occur at any of these points, an illness or event whatsoever threatens the life at that age. [Thus, for instance, say a break occurs on a Line of Life at the point where you see the figure 40, you may predict an illness at that age, or say the line ceases abruptly at the point 55, you may predict the death of the subject at that age.] It has often been objected that it is difficult to divide the line in a living hand from a diagram like Plate XI., owing to the difference in the size; but the difficulty ought not to exist, for the circumference of the Mount of Venus

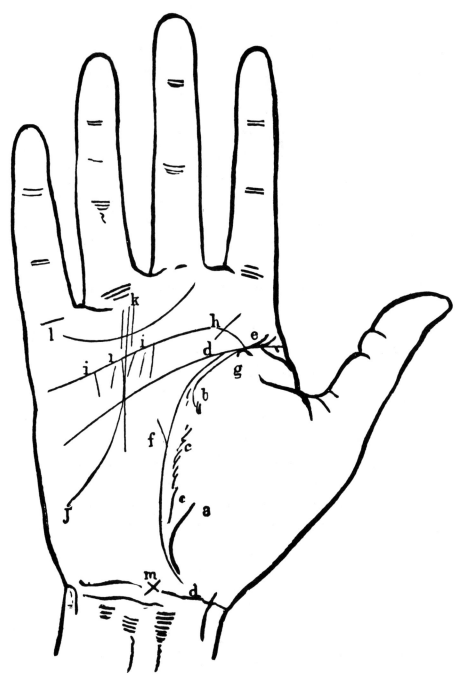

PLATE XII.—MODIFICATIONS OF THE PRINCIPAL LINES.

has only to be divided [mentally] into eighteen equal parts, the points of division of which should be taken to represent the ages indicated on the diagram. A little experience will render this mental operation quite easy.

The shorter the line the shorter the life, and from the point at which the line terminates in both hands, may be predicted accurately the time at which death will supervene.

421.
Short line, short life.

A break in the line denotes always an illness. If the line is broken in both hands, there is great danger of death, *especially* if the lower branch of the break turn inwards towards the Mount of Venus [as at *a*, in Plate XII.], and the sign is repeated in *both* hands.

422.
Breaks in the line.

And here it is well to impress upon the readers a point of vital importance ; that is, the absolute necessity to bear in mind that to be *certain* a sign *must* be repeated in *both* hands ; and this applies particularly and especially to the indications of accident and disease upon the Line of Life. A break in one hand, and not in the other, betokens *only* a danger of illness ; and in like manner, if in one hand the line stop short at say 35, death cannot be predicted at that age, unless it also stop short at the same point in the other. These things must be very carefully learnt before they are put into practice, for to make a deliberate statement as regards the above, would be a brutal and dangerous thing to do, unless one spoke with *absolute* certainty.

423.
Necessity of corroborative signs in *both* hands.

The line ceasing abruptly with a few little parallel lines, as at *b* in Plate XII., is an indication of sudden death. If the line is continually crossed by little cutting bars, it is an indication of continual, but not severe, illnesses.

424.
Sudden death.

If the line is broken up and laddered, as at *cc* in Plate XII., it denotes a period of continued delicacy and ill-health. If it is broken inside a square, as at *a* in Plate XIII., it indicates recovery from a

425.
Broken line. Square.

8

serious illness ; a square *always* denotes protection from some danger [564]. A bar across the broken ends [as at *b*, Plate XIII.] also denotes a preservation from an illness.

426.
Sister line.

Whatever may be the condition of the line, a sister line, as at *ad*, Plate XII., will replace it and counteract the evil effects of the irregularities found on the main line, protect the subject against most of the dangers which assail him, and indicate a luxurious, comfortable existence.

427.
Forked or tasselled.

The line should be free from forks and tassels throughout its course. Tasselled at its extremity, as at *c* in Plate XIII., it indicates poverty and loss of money late in life, if not earlier. Forked at the commencement, as at *e*, Plate XII., it indicates vanity, indecision, and fantasy ; but if the fork is very clear and simple [not confused as in the figure], it may in a good hand mean justice of soul and fidelity. In like manner, if instead of the tassel at *c*, Plate XIII., we find a plain fork, it points to overwork in old age resulting in poverty ; it is, in fact, the first warning of the appearance of the tassel. A ray of the tassel going to the Mount of the Moon [as at *d*, Plate XIII.] shows a great danger of folly resulting from these troubles. A fork going to the Line of Head [as at *e*, Plate XIII.] equals faithfulness, but if it be at the side of the hand, as at *f*, it is, on the contrary, a sign of inconstancy. A fork in the very centre of the line is a warning of diminished force, which *must* be attended by a relaxation of the efforts, especially if the tassel appears at the base of the line, or the head is at all weak.

428.
Rays across the hand.
Worry lines.

Rays across the hand from the Mount of Venus [as in Plate XIV.] always denote worries and troubles. Across the Line of Fortune to a star in the Triangle, they denote loss of money ; continued to the Line of Head, as at *b*, a ray indicates a consequent loss of reason, or, at any rate, danger to the mental faculties. Cutting the Line of Apollo, as at *c*, it betokens a worry or loss of money early in

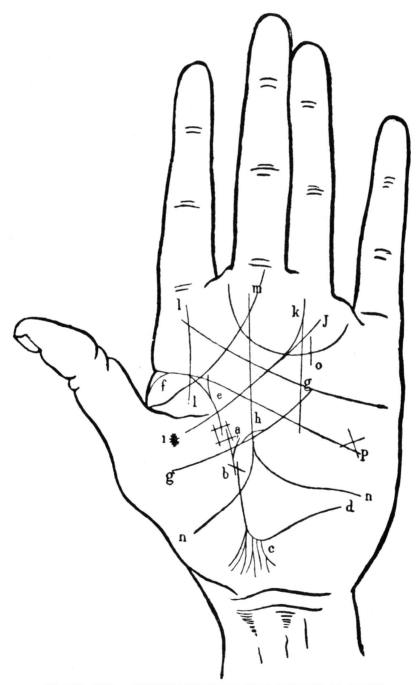

PLATE XIII.—MODIFICATIONS OF THE PRINCIPAL LINES.

life, by reason of the ruin or misfortune of one's parents; if it starts from a star, as at *d*, it shows that the misfortune was caused by the death of a parent. The age at which these troubles occur is shown by the place at which the Line of Life is cut by the worry line. If the worry line terminates at a point or star upon the Lines of Head or Heart [as from *f*, in Plate XIV.], or upon the Mount of Mars, it denotes that the worry has brought about an illness. If the line goes straight to the heart, as at *gg*, in Plate XIII., it indicates an unhappy love affair; if an island appear in the line [*h*, Plate XIII.], the consequences are likely to be, or have been, serious, if not shameful; a fork at the point where *gg* cuts the Line of Life, as in Plate XIII., indicates an unhappy marriage, or even a divorce. A worry line from a star in the mount [*i*, Plate XIII.] indicates quarrels with relations, ending in ruin if it goes up to the Mount of Apollo, as at *j*; but if it goes up and joins with the Line of Apollo, as at *k*, it is a prognostic of good fortune arising therefrom. A line from the Mount of Venus, *just* cutting the Line of Life, as at *h* in Plate XIV, indicates marriage at the age whereat the line is found.

429. Rays cutting the Line of Life. Rays across the hand just cutting the line, generally indicate an illness caused by the mount or line whence the ray takes its departure, at the age at which it occurs upon the line; thus, from the Line of Heart it means an illness caused by the heart; from the Line of Head an illness caused by the head or brain; from the Mount of Mars a danger brought about by passion, and so on.

430. Ray up to ♃. A ray ascending to the Mount of Jupiter, as at *ll* in Plate XIII., betrays ambition, lofty aims, egoism, and success. These lines often appear in a hand quite suddenly.

431. Spots on the line. If a branch rise from a black spot on the line, it indicates that a disease has left a nervous complaint. Black spots always indicate diseases, and if they are very deep, they indicate sudden death.

432.
Ascending
and
descending
branches.

Branches ascending from the line, as in Plate XV., denote ambition, and nearly always riches; if they ascend *through* the other lines, as at *a a a*, they indicate that the success is brought about by the personal merit of the subject. *Descending* branches, as at *b*, Plate XV., denote loss of health and wealth.

433.
Starting
under ♃.

If instead of starting from the extreme outside of the hand, the Line of Life commences under the Mount of Jupiter [say at *g*, Plate XII.], it betrays great ambition, and is often a sign of great successes and honors.

434.
Joined to
Head and
Heart.

If the Lines of Life, Head, and Heart are *all* joined *together* at the commencement, it is a terrible sign of misfortune and violent death.

435.
Cross and
branches.

A cross cut by branches of the line, as at *c*, Plate XV., betokens a mortal infirmity, with grave fear of death; a cross at the end of the line, as at *d*, denotes [if the line is otherwise clear] that the subject will suffer unmerited reverses in his old age. A cross at the commencement of the line indicates an accident in early life, especially if a point be also found on the line at the same place.

436.
Line from ♂.

A line from the Mount of Mars cutting the Line of Life, as at *ee* in Plate XV., indicates a wound.

437.
Ray to ☉.

A ray going direct from the line to the Mount of Apollo, denotes celebrity; if it is indistinct, this celebrity is obstructed by some quality of the character, which must be sought for and guarded against.

438.
Spots and
circles.

Spots upon the line are indications of temporary illness, while circles denote a serious affection of the eyes, often resulting in blindness.

439.
Separate
from head.

If the line, instead of being joined to the Line of Head, be separated, as at *f* in Plate XV., it is a sign of folly and carelessness, of extreme self-reliance and foolhardiness in consequence, especially if

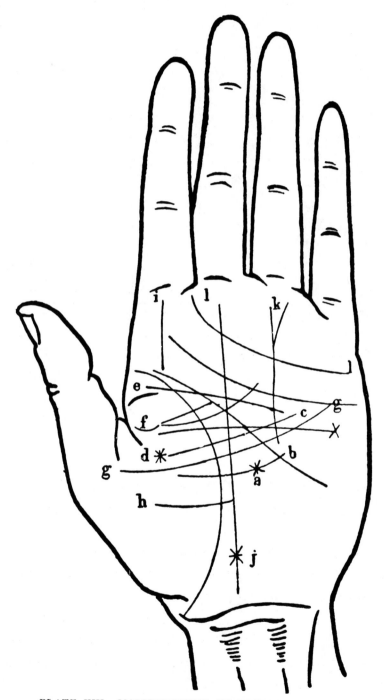

PLATE XIV.—MODIFICATIONS OF PRINCIPAL LINES.

the space be filled with a mesh of little lines, and the lines themselves be big and red.

If the line come out in a great circle into the palm of the hand, and reach, or end, close to the Mount of the Moon, it is a sign of long life.   If a line have a break in it *and* a sister line, the latter mends it, as it were, and the only effect of the break is a delicacy during the period over which the break extends.   If the broken end of the line join with the Line of Fortune, it is an indication that, at some time or other, the life has been in great danger, from which it has been protected by good luck.

440. Curving out to Mount of ☽.

Again, if the line appears to be short, an intense desire to live, supported by a strong phalanx of will and a good Line of Head, will often prolong it, the prolongation being marked on the hand by the appearance of sister lines or capillaries.

441. Short line contracted.

A Line of Life lying close to the thumb is a mark of sterility, especially if the Lines of Health and Head are joined by a star.

442. Close to thumb.

An island [573–78] on the line denotes an illness during the period of its length, generally caused by some excess shown elsewhere on the hand.   If the line of health is absent, the island denotes biliousness and indigestion ; an island at the very commencement of the line betrays some mystery of birth, some fatality, or some hereditary disease.

443. Island.

CHAPTER II.

The Line of Mars.

444.
Effects of
the line.

In some hands we find inside the line of life, and running parallel and close to it, a second or sister line known in cheirosophy as the Line of Mars, or the Martial Line [Plate VII.]. Like all sister lines, it repairs and mitigates the effects of breaks in the main line ; and it derives its name from the fact that it gives to soldiers great successes in arms, especially if it is clear and red in color.

445.
Indications.

It gives, together with riches and prosperity, a great heat and violence to the passions, which with this line, if uncontrolled, are apt to become brutish. Its influence lasts throughout the period during which it follows the Line of Life.

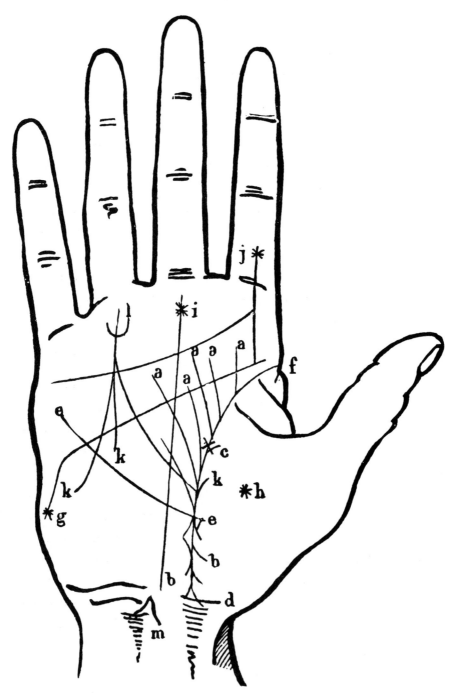

PLATE XV.—MODIFICATIONS OF THE PRINCIPAL LINES.

CHAPTER III.

The Line of Heart.

THIS line should be neat, well colored, and extending from the Mount of Jupiter to the outside of the hand under the Mount of Mercury, not broad and pale, or thick and red, but well traced, and of a good normal color ; such a condition of the line indicates a good heart, an affectionate disposition, with an equable temper and good health.

446.
Proper aspects.

The strength of the affection is in proportion to the length of the line ; if the line, instead of beginning at the Mount of Jupiter, begins upon the Mount of Saturn, the subject will be more sensual than Platonic in his affections.

447.
Length of the line.

Traced right across the hand [from side to side], it indicates an excess of affection which produces jealousy and suffering in consequence thereof, especially if the Mount of the Moon is high.

448.
Excess.

If it is chained in its formation, the subject is an inveterate flirt, and, unless the rest of the hand be very strong, will be much subject to palpitations of the heart.

449.
Chained.

Bright red in color, the line denotes violence in affairs of the heart, and, on the other hand, a pale line, broad and chained, betrays a cold-blooded *roué*, if not a condition of heart utterly *blasé*. A livid or yellow color betrays subjection to liver complaints.

450.
Color.

The line should be close underneath, well up to the bases of the mounts ; a line which lies close to that of the head throughout its length, betrays evil instincts, avarice, envy, hypocrisy, and duplicity.

451.
Position.

452.
Commencing under ♄.

A Line of Heart which begins quite suddenly without branches or rays beneath the Mount of Saturn, foreshadows a short life and a sudden death. If the line is very thin and runs right across the hand, it indicates cruelty even to murderous instincts.

453.
Between first and second fingers.

If the line, instead of terminating on the Mounts of Jupiter or Saturn, seems to disappear between the first and second fingers, it betokens a long life of unremitting labor.

454.
Girdle of ♀ and ☽.

If to a large Line of Heart a subject add the Girdle of Venus [Plate VII.] and a high Mount of the Moon, he will be a victim to the most unreasoning jealousy.

455.
Absence of the line

If in a hand there be found *no* Line of Heart, it is an unfailing sign of treachery, hypocrisy, and the worst instincts, and, unless the Line of Health be very good, the subject will be liable to heart disease, and runs a grave danger of a sudden, early death.

455a.
Breaks in the line.

A line which is much broken up denotes inconstancy, and often these subjects are woman-haters. A single break shows a feebleness of the heart, and the cause of that feebleness may always be found in some excess or evil development of a mount—fatality shown by a development of the Mount of Saturn ; foolishness shown by an equal development of the Mounts of Saturn and Apollo ; pride shown by the Mount of Apollo ; folly or avarice shown by the Mount of Mercury.

456.
Many little lines.

A quantity of little lines cutting across the line diagonally indicates many misfortunes of the heart, arising originally from weakness of the heart or liver.

457.
Forked.

The line dividing at the end and going in three branches to the Mount of Jupiter, is a most fortunate sign, indicating riches and good-luck. Any forking of the line which sends a branch on to the Mount of Jupiter is good ; even if the branch goes to between the fingers of Jupiter and Saturn, this betokens still good fortune, but of a more quiet and undisturbing description. But a forking which sends one ray upon the Mount of Jupiter and the other upon the Mount of Saturn, betrays errors and failures in the search after success, and fanaticism in religion.

If the line is quite bare under the finger of Jupiter at its commencement, there is great danger of poverty; a similar bareness at the percussion indicates sterility; the fork under Jupiter gives also to the subject energy and enthusiasm in love. A line quite bare of branches throughout its length indicates dryness of heart and want of affection.

458.
Bare line.

If the line touch the base of the finger of Jupiter, the subject will be unsuccessful in all his undertakings, unless the Line of Fortune be exceptionally good.

459.
Touching ♃.

A mark like a deep scar across the line betrays a tendency to apoplexy; red spots or holes in the line denote wounds either physical or moral. White marks on the line denote conquests in love; a point on the line means grief of the heart, and, according to its position, you can tell by whom it was caused, thus: Under the Mount of Apollo the cause was an artist, or a celebrity—*i.e.*, the grief is connected with art or ambition; under the Mount of Mercury the grief is caused by a man of science, a lawyer, or a doctor.

460.
Marks on the line.

If the line curl round the first finger, it is a sign of a marvellous faculty for occultism and the possession of high occult powers.

461.
Curled round first finger.

Joined to the Line of Head under the Mounts of Jupiter or Saturn, it is a sign of a great danger threatening the life, and of sudden and violent death if the sign is repeated in both hands. If the line turn down on to the Line of Head, with a ray across it, as at *h* in Plate XII., it is a sign of a miserable marriage, or deep griefs of the heart.

462.
Joined to head.

A ray from the Line of Life to the Mount of Saturn, reaching to the base of the finger [as at *m* in Plate XIII.], is a very bad sign in

463.
Ray to ♄.

a woman's hand, immeasurably and even fatally increasing the dangers of maternity.

464.
Lines from the quad-rangle.

Lines from the Quadrangle to the Line of Heart, as at *i i i* in Plate XII., denote aptitude for science, curiosity, research, and versatility, which often culminates in uselessness.

465.
Curved line to ☽.

A curved line from the Line of Heart to the Mount of the Moon [stopping *abruptly* at the Line of Heart (395)], as at *j* in Plate XII., denotes murderous tendencies and instincts.

CHAPTER IV.

The Line of Head.

THIS line should be joined to the Line of Life at its immediate commencement, and leaving it directly should trace a strong ray across the hand to the top of the Mount of the Moon, clear and well colored, without ramifications or forking, uninterrupted and regular; such a formation indicates good sense, clear judgment, cleverness, and strength of will.

466. Proper aspects.

Pale and broad, it indicates feebleness or want of intellect. Short—*i.e.*, reaching only to the Plain of Mars,—it betrays weak ideas and weak will. [Stopping under the Mount of Saturn, it foreshadows an early, sudden death.] Chained, it betrays a want of fixity of ideas and vacillation of mind. Long and very thin, it denotes treachery and infidelity. Of unequal thickness, twisted, and badly colored, it betrays a feeble liver and want of spirit; such subjects are always avaricious.

467. Evil conditions and aspects.

A long Line of Head gives domination to a character—*i.e.*, domination of self as opposed to the domination of others, indicated by a large thumb. A long Line of Head in a many-rayed and lined hand gives great self-control and coolness in dangers and difficulties, and the strength of the head [shown by the long line] causes the subject to reason out and utilize the intuitive powers and instinctive promptings indicated by the multiplicity of rays and lines in the hand.

468. Length of the line.

Very long and straight—*i.e.*, cutting the entire hand in a straight line from the Line of Life to the percussion,—it indicates excess of

469. Excessive length.

reasoning habits, over-calculation, and over-economy, denoting avarice and meanness.

470.
Modifica-
tions.
The excessive economy [avarice] of this long line may be greatly
modified by a softness of the hand or a high development of the
Mounts of Jupiter or of Apollo.

471.
Starting un-
der ♄.
If instead of joining the Line of Life at its commencement it only
leaves it under the Mount of Saturn, it is a sure indication that the
education has been acquired and the brain developed late in life;
or, if the Line of Life is short, and the Line of Head also, it foreshadows a grave danger of sudden death. A like commencement,
the line reaching across to the Mount of Mars, the Line of Heart
being thin and small, indicates struggles and misfortunes arising
from infirmities of temper or errors of calculation, unless the Line of
Fortune is exceptionally good. Such a subject will often appear
benevolent, but his benevolence will generally be found to be only
of a nature which gives pleasure to himself, and is usually more
theoretical than practical.

472.
Position.
The line must lie at a good regular distance from that of the
heart; lying close up to it throughout its length, it betrays weakness and palpitations of the organ.

473.
Influence of
good line.
Remember that an extremely good Line of Head may so influence
the whole hand as to dominate over evil signs which may there be
found, especially if the Mount of Mars be also high; such a combination gives to a subject energy, circumspection, constancy, coolness, and a power of resistance which goes a long way towards com-
bating any evil or weak tendencies which may be found in his
hand.

474.
Stopped un-
der ♄ or ☉.
If the line stops abruptly under the Mount of Saturn, it forewarns
of a cessation of the intelligence, or [with other signs] death in early
youth; stopping similarly under the finger of Apollo, it betrays
inconstancy in the ideas and a want of order in the mind.

If, though visible, it appears joined to the Line of Life for some way before leaving it to go across the hand, it indicates timidity and want of confidence, which give dulness and apathy to the life, and which are with difficulty overcome. When this sign appears in an otherwise clever hand, the most strenuous efforts should be made to counteract this want of self-reliance, which is so serious an obstacle to success. Joined to the Line of Life in a really *strong* and clever hand, the indication will be of caution and circumspection.

475. Joined to Life at commencement.

Thin in the centre for a short space, the line indicates a nervous illness, neuralgia, or some kindred disease.

476. Thin at centre.

Separated from the Line of Life at its commencement and going well across the hand, it indicates intelligence, self-reliance, and spontaneity [439], and, with a long thumb, ambition. Separate from the Line of Life, and short or weak, it betrays carelessness, fantasy, jealousy, and deceit ; often these subjects have bad sight. Separated thus, but connected by branches or ramifications, it indicates evil temper and capriciousness ; connected by a cross, it betrays domestic troubles and discomforts. Even in a good hand there is danger in this sign of *brusquerie,* and a too great promptitude of decision which often leads to error. With the Mounts of Saturn or Mars prominently developed, it is a sign of great audacity or imprudence, but it is a useful prognostic [within limits] for public characters or actors, giving them enthusiasm and boldness of manner in public, and the gift of eloquence by reason of their self-confidence. A *long* line thus separated will give want of tact and discrimination, and an impulsive manner of speech, which is often inconvenient, and sometimes wounds.

477. Separated from the Line of Life.

If the line, instead of going straight across the hand to the base of the Mount of Mars or to the top of the Mount of the Moon, trace an oblique course to a termination *on* the Mount of the Moon, it is a sign of idealism, imagination, and want of instinct of real life. If

478. Declining to the Mount of ☽.

it comes very low upon the mount, it leads to mysticism and folly, even culminating in madness if the Line of Health is cut by it in both hands.   In an otherwise fairly strong hand this declension upon the Mount of the Moon gives poetry and a love of the mystic or occult sciences, superstition, and an inclination to spiritualism. Such a formation, if the Mount of the Moon is rayed, generally gives a talent for literature.   The Line of Head coming low upon the Mount of the Moon to a star, as at *g* in Plate XV., with stars on the Mounts of Venus and Saturn, as at *h* and *i*, and a weak Line of Heart, are terribly certain signs of hereditary madness.   This extreme obliquity of the line always indicates a *danger* of madness, and these concomitant signs [314] prove it to be hereditary, and probably unavoidable.

479.
Turning up
to a mount.
  Again, if instead of going across the hand it turn up towards one of the mounts, it will show that the thoughts are entirely taken up by the qualities belonging to the respective mounts; thus turning up to the Mount of Mercury, commerce will be the prevailing instinct, and will bring good fortune; or, turning towards the Mount of Apollo, a desire for reputation will be the continual thought.   If it point between the fingers of Apollo and Mercury, the signification is of success in art brought by scientific treatment. If the line go right up on to the mount, it will denote a folly of the quality—thus, for instance, ending on Mercury it will denote occultism and deceit; on Apollo, the mania of art; and on Saturn, the mania of religion.

480.
Turning up
to, or cutting, Heart.
  Any turning up of the Line of Head towards that of the heart denotes a weak mind, which lets his heart and his passions domineer over his reason; if it *touch* the Line of Heart, it is a prognostic of early death.   If it cut through the Line of Heart and end upon the Mount of Saturn, it foreshadows death from a wound to the head. If it turn up to the Line of Heart and confound itself with it

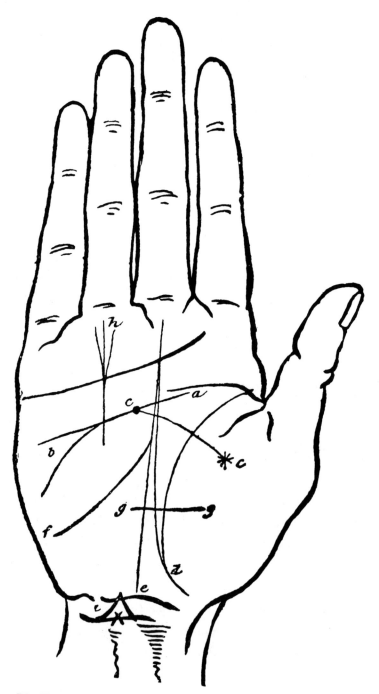

PLATE XVI.—MODIFICATIONS OF THE PRINCIPAL LINES.

obliquely, it foreshadows a fatal affection, which runs a great risk of terminating in madness.

Turning back towards the thumb, the Line of Head denotes intense egotism and misfortune in consequence thereof.

481. Turning back.

A break in the Line of Head nearly always indicates an injury to the head. Broken under the finger of Saturn, and the broken ends overlapping, as at *a* in Plate XVI., the prognostic is especially certain, but in a bad hand it is said to be a sign of the scaffold, or, at any rate, of the loss of a member, *even* if the sign appear in one hand only. Much broken up, it is a sign of headaches and general weakness of the head, resulting in loss of memory and want of continuity in the ideas. Such a breaking up will rob a long phalanx of will of much of its power, and long fingers of much of their spirit of minutiæ. If with this shattered Line of the Head we find in the Plain of Mars a cross, the rays terminating in points or spots and short nails, it is a grave warning of a tendency to epilepsy.

482. Breaks in the line.

Cross in ♂.

Split throughout its length is a strengthening sign if other indications of madness appear in the hand, but if the line is distinctly *double* [*i.e.*, if it is accompanied by a sister line] it is a sure sign of good fortune and inheritances.

483. Split and sister line.

If the line is forked at the end, with one of the "prongs" descending upon the Mount of the Moon [as at *b* in Plate XVI.], we have a certain indication of lying, hypocrisy, and deceit. Such a man, even with a good hand, will be a clever sophist, never off his guard, ready at all times with [if necessary] an ingenious rearrangement of facts to suit the needs of the immediate present. This forking has somewhat the effect of short nails, giving to a subject a love of controversy and argument. If the rays or "prongs" of the fork are so long that one extends right across the hand, and the other comes well down to the rascette, it has the dual effect of a long Line of Head, and of a Line of Head which descends far upon the

484. Forked at the end.

Mount of the Moon, giving at once poetry and realism—*i.e.*, a capability of making a practical use of poetic inspirations. A good Line of Apollo gives *great* talent to a forked Line of Head, from its power of seeing all round a subject, and of considering it from all points. If one ray of the fork go up to touch the Line of Heart, and the other descend upon the Mount of the Moon, it betrays the sacrifice of all things to an affection, and if with this sign the Line of Saturn or Fortune stop short at the Line of the Heart, it denotes that this infatuation has brought ruin with it. The two signs are nearly always concomitant.

485.
Cut by lines.

Cut by a multitude of little lines, the Line of Head indicates a short life, with many illnesses and headaches. If the little cross lines are confined to the middle of the Line of Head, it is a sign of dishonesty.

486.
Cross.

A cross in the middle of the line is a foreshadowing of near approaching death, or of a mortal wound if the line is also broken at this point.

487.
Points on the line.

Red points indicate wounds; white ones indicate discoveries in science or inventions; black points, ailments according to the mount most developed in the hand. Thus with the Mount of Saturn, toothaches; with the Mount of Venus, deafness; with the Mount of Apollo, diseases of the eyes [especially if a star appear at the junction of the finger of Apollo and the palm]. These points are often connected with similar spots on the Line of Life by rays or lines, which enable us to pronounce with certainty the ages at which the subject has suffered from these maladies.

488.
Knotted.

A knotting up of the line betrays an impulse to murder, which, if the knot is pale, is past, but which, if the knot is deep red, is to come.

489.
Capillaries.

Capillary lines [Fig. 9, Plate VIII.] on the Line of Head are a sign of a well-ordered mind and a good disposition.

An island in the Line of Head is an indication of acutely sensitive nerves.

A star upon the line is generally a sign of a very bad wound, bringing danger of folly with it.

If a line be found connecting a star on the Mount of Venus with a spot on the Line of Head [as at *cc* in Plate XVI.], it indicates a deeply rooted and ever-remembered disappointment in love.

If a line extend from the Line of Head to the root of the finger of Jupiter [as at *i* in Plate XIV.], it indicates intense pride and vanity which is easily wounded ; if it end at a star upon the finger [as at *j* in Plate XV.], it is a sign of extreme good-luck; but if it end at the same place by a cross, the luck will be, on the contrary, extremely bad. This little line, joined by the Line of Saturn, or Fortune, indicates vanity, reaching even to folly.

CHAPTER V.

The Line of Saturn, or Fortune.

494.
Its points of departure and their indications.
THE Line of Saturn, or Fortune, has three principal points of departure for its base: it may start from the Line of Life, as at *d* in Plate XVI.; from the *rascette*, as at *e;* or from the Mount of the Moon, as at *f.* Starting from the Line of Life, the Line of Fortune indicates that the luck in life is the result of one's own personal merit. If it start from the wrist, or rascette, the fortune will be very good, especially if it trace a fine, strong furrow on the Mount of Saturn; in the same direction, but commencing higher up from a point in the Plain of Mars, we get an indication of a painful, troubled life, especially if the line penetrate [as it often does] into the finger. If the line start from the Mount of the Moon, it shows [if it goes straight to the Mount of Saturn] that the fortune is, to a great extent, derived from the caprice of the opposite sex. If from the Mount of the Moon the line go to that of the heart, and, confounding itself therein, go on up to the Mount of Jupiter, it is an infallible sign of a rich and fortunate marriage. You must guard against confounding a chance line from the Mount of the Moon to the Line of Saturn with the Line of Saturn starting from that mount. If [besides the Line of Saturn, as at *e* in Plate XVI.] we have another line starting as at *f*, in Plate XVI., and *cutting* instead of joining the Line of Saturn, it betrays the fatal effects of imagination, culminating possibly in weakness, or evil to the mental capacity. Starting from the very base of the Mount of the Moon, and ending on the Mount of Saturn, is an indication of prediction and clairvoyance.

Instead of going to the Mount of Saturn, the line may go up to some other mount, in which case it will have special significations; thus, going to the Mount of Mercury, we get fortune in commerce, eloquence, and science; going to the Mount of Apollo, we get fortune from art or wealth; going to the Mount of Jupiter, we find satisfied pride, and the attainment of the objects of our ambition.

495. Termination of the line.

If the line, instead of stopping on the mount, go right up to the second joint of the finger, we have the indication of very great fortune, which will be either very good or very bad, according to the concomitant signs. Thus, with a good hand, this is a first-rate sign; but with a deep red line on the mount, and a star on the first phalanx of the finger, we have the indication of the worst possible fortune, ending in a violent death, probably on the scaffold. The line should just extend from the top of the rascette to the centre of the Mount of Saturn; reaching to the jointure of the finger and palm, or penetrating into the rascette is a bad sign, being a sure indication of misery. Starting from the rascette, and stopped at the Line of Heart, indicates a misfortune arising from a disappointment in love; or, in a weak hand, heart disease. Similarly stopped at the Line of Head, the misfortune will arise from an error of calculation, or from an illness of the head.

496. Length of the line.

Stopped at Lines of Head or Heart.

If it only *start* from the Line of Head it denotes labor, pain, and ill-health, unless the Line of Head is very good, when it will be an indication of fortune acquired late in life by the intelligence of the subject. Shorter still—*i.e.*, from the quadrangle to the Mount of Saturn—the indications are still more unfortunate, being of great sorrows, and even of imprisonment. The evil prognostications of a line which goes into the third phalanx of the finger of Saturn may be averted by the presence of a square [564] on the mount.

497. Starting short.

498.
Broken in quadrangle.

If the line is stopped in the quadrangle, and then starts again at the Line of Heart, ending its course upon the mount, it denotes that though the luck will be obstructed and retarded, it will not be permanently spoilt, and the position in life will not be lost ; and this is especially certain if a good Line of Apollo be found in the hand.

499.
Age on the Line of Fate.

And this brings us to the indications of age on the Line of Saturn. The line starts from its base, and on it [as in Plate XI.] one can tell by its breaks, and so on, approximately the ages at which events have occurred in a life ; it must, however, be premised that these indications are not anything like as sure as those of the Line of Life. From the base of the line to the Line of Head we have thirty years, from the Line of Head to that of the heart we find the events of the life between thirty and forty-five years, and thence to the top of the line takes us to the end of the life. Thus, for instance, if you see a gap, or break, in the line from the Line of Head to just below the Line of Heart, you can predict misfortunes between the ages of thirty and forty ; and a connecting line will generally indicate the nature and cause of the ill-luck. Also it will often be found that in the right hand a misfortune will be marked on the Line of Saturn, the exact *date* of which will be marked by a point on the line in the left hand.

500.
Explanations by ♄.

The indications found upon the Line of Saturn often explain and elucidate indications only dimly or vaguely traced upon the Line of Life, or in the rest of the hand.

501.
Conditions of the line.
Twisted.

A perfectly straight line, with branches going upwards from its two sides, indicates a gradual progress from poverty to riches. Twisted at the base, and straight at the top, indicates early misfortunes, followed by good-luck. Straightness, and good color, from the Line of Heart upwards, always betokens good fortune in old age, with invention in science, and talent for such pursuits as

Split.

horticulture, agriculture, construction, and architecture. Split and twisted, the Line of Saturn indicates ill-health from an abuse of pleasure. A twisted condition of the line always denotes quarrels, and a very good and well-traced Line of Saturn will annul the evil indications of a badly formed Line of Life.

A broken and ragged condition of the line betrays an inconstancy and changeability of fortune. Breaks in the line in the Plain of Mars denote physical and moral struggles. Even, however, if it is broken up, it may be replaced by a very good development of the Mount of Saturn, or a favorable aspect of the Mount of Mars ; and to the worst luck a high Mount of the Moon will give a calm and resignation which rob it of much of its evil indication. A strong, irregular Line of Fortune, in a much-rayed and lined hand, betrays a constant irritability and a supersensitive condition of mind. A well-traced Line of Saturn always gives a long life ; broken up at the base is an indication of misery in early life, up to the age [499] at which the breaking up ceases. If it end in a star on the mount, it foreshadows great misfortune, following great good-luck ; in a good hand this sign generally means that the misfortune is caused by the fault of others, *generally* of one's relations. For the Line of Saturn to be lucky, there must be explanatory points in the hand for the luck to come from, and to find these is one of the most important tasks of the cheirosophist.

502.
Breaks in the line.

Cut by a multitude of little lines on the mount, we can safely foretell misfortunes late in life, after a long period of good-luck. Cut by a line starting from the Mount of Venus, it denotes conjugal misery, or misfortune caused by a woman [*gg*, in Plate XVI.].

503.
Cut by lines.

If the line is simply absent from a hand, it denotes an insignificant life, which takes things as they come, meeting with neither particularly good nor particularly bad fortune.

504.
Absence.

Forked, with one ray going to the Mount of Venus and the other to the Mount of the Moon [as at *nn* in Plate XIII.], we find a strife

505.
Forked.

for success, directed by the wildest imagination, and spurred on by love. If the line go well up, as in Plate XIII., the ambition will be successful, after much struggle ; but if the main line is broken or malformed, the necessary intrigues and caprices caused by the formation of the line will result in inevitable misfortune.

506.
Crosses.

Any cross upon the line indicates a change of position or of prospects in life at the age indicated by the position of the cross upon the line [as in Plate XI.]. In the very centre of the line it is always a misfortune, and the cause of it may nearly always be found upon the Lines of Head or Life, showing the misfortune to arise from error or miscalculation, or from illness or the loss of friends.

507.
Stars.

A star at the base of the line [as at *j* in Plate XIV.] denotes a loss of fortune, brought by the parents of the subject in early youth ; if there be also a star on the Mount of Venus [as at *h* in Plate XV.], the immediate cause is the early death of a parent.

508.
Island.

An island on the line betrays, *almost invariably*, a conjugal infidelity ; a star accompanying the island betokens a great misfortune arising therefrom. At the very base of a line, an island indicates a mystery connected with the birth of the subject, and with this sign an extreme malformation of the line will betray illegitimacy. In a really good hand, an island on the Line of Saturn indicates a hopeless, untold passion ; with a star and a cross on the Mount of Jupiter, the island will show that the passion has been for a celebrated or exalted person.

CHAPTER VI.

The Line of Apollo, or Brilliancy.

THE Line of Brilliancy may start either from the Line of Life, the Plain of Mars, or the Mount of the Moon, as at *k k k* in Plate XV. Whenever it is present, it denotes glory, celebrity, art, wealth, merit, or success; its best aspect is when it is neat and straight, making a clear cut upon the Mount of Apollo, signifying celebrity in art, and consequent riches, with a capacity for enjoying and making the best of them. Clearly marked, the line also denotes that the subject is under the favor or influence of the great; it gives him, also, the calmness of natural talent, and the contentment of self-approbation.

509. Position in the hand.

It is necessary that this line exist in a really lucky hand to make its good fortune absolute; a good Line of Saturn will be seriously compromised by the absence of this line.

510. Necessity in lucky hand.

With the Mounts of Jupiter and Mercury developed, this line is a certain indication of wealth, and such a subject will become celebrated by his fortune, dignity, and merit, no less than by his talents and scientific capacities.

511. With ♃ and ☿.

Twisted fingers, or a hollow palm, are very bad signs with this line; for they show that the influences of the line are guided in an evil direction, and that the talents betokened by it are used for the attainment of bad ends.

512. Twisted fingers.

With a long Line of Head, and a long finger of Apollo, the tendencies of the line will be material, the ambition and talents being turned towards the attainment of riches.

513. With long Head and ☉.

514.
Proper aspects of the line.
The line, to have all its highest artistic significations, should be well colored ; pale, it denotes that the subject is not actively artistic, but has merely the instincts of art, loving things that are brilliant and beautiful. In these respects the indications are the same as those of a high Mount of Apollo *without* the line ; such a formation also gives a love of the beautiful *without* production, the mount giving the instincts, and the line giving the talents, of art.

515.
Absence.
Absence of the line from a hand indicates want of success in projects and undertakings which would lead to glory and success.

Broken up.
Much broken up, it indicates a Jack-of-all-trades and an eccentricity in art which renders it of little avail to the owner.

516.
Lined
Mount of ⊙.
Many little lines upon the mount point generally to an excess of artistic instinct, which generally falls by its own weight, and comes to nothing ; it is much better to have only one line on the mount, unless all are equally clear and well traced. With two or three lines, a subject will often follow two or three different branches of art, without succeeding particularly in any one.

517.
Signs in the quadrangle.
If the line is confused and split up in the quadrangle, but clear above, we find misfortunes, having, however, good terminations. Any signs upon the Line of Apollo in the quadrangle must be carefully observed, for they always denote worries, and are generally connected by a worry-line [428] with the Line of Life and Mount of Venus, showing the times at which they occurred.

518.
Divided on the mount.
If the line is equally divided on the mount, as at *k* in Plate XIV., we find an equal balancing of two instincts, which ends in a nullity in the matter of art. Divided into a curved trident, as at *l* in Plate XV., it is a sure indication of vast unrealized desires of wealth ; if, however, the line divides into a pointed trident from the Line of Heart, as at *h* in Plate XVI., we can safely announce future glory, riches, and celebrity arising from personal merit ; and if, instead of being joined at the Heart, the three lines rise parallel and

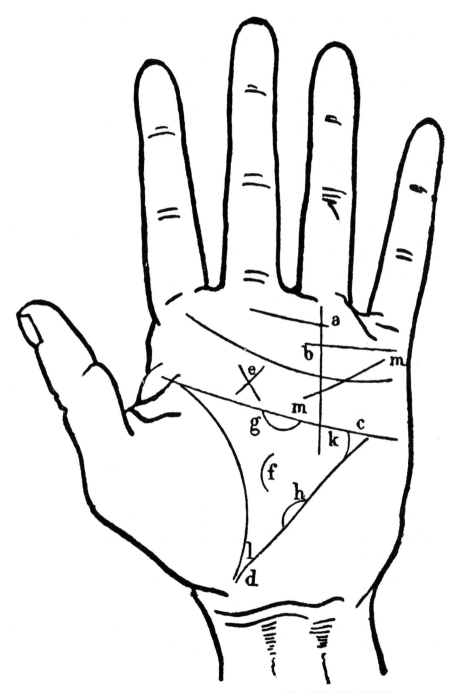

PLATE XVII.—THE QUADRANGLE AND THE TRIANGLE.

identical, as at *k* in Plate XII., tracing three fine troughs on the mount, we have these same indications intensified and made yet more certain.

Cross-lines on the mount are obstacles which stand in the way of artistic success, very often arising from the envy and malignity of others. **519.** Cross-lines.

Cut by a line coming from the Mount of Saturn, as at *a* in Plate XVII., poverty will stand in the way of complete success. Similarly cut by a line coming from the Mount of Mercury, as at *b* in Plate XVII., the success and good fortune will be marred and prevented by inconstancy and changeableness of spirit. **520.** Lines from ♄ and ☿.

A star on the mount is a good sign, indicating success and good-luck, arising from the favor of others and the help of friends. **521.** Star.

A cross upon the mount *close to* the line, or even touching it, denotes instinct of religion and piety. **522.** Cross.

A black spot at the junction of the Lines of Heart and of Apollo betrays a great danger, if not an imminent peril of blindness. **523.** Spot.

CHAPTER VII.

The Line of Liver, or Health.

524.
Position in the hand.

THE position which the liver line [Line of Health, or *hepatica*] occupies in the hand may be seen by looking at the Map of the Hand, Plate VII., but it will strike the cheirosophist, after very little experience, that this line fully developed in a hand is comparatively scarce, and the reason of this is the comparatively unhealthy lives which the majority of people live nowadays.

525
Proper aspects.

Long, clearly traced, and well colored and proportioned, the line denotes good health, gayety, a clear conscience, and success in life. If it is lengthened up to the upper part of the palm, it is a sign that the good health of the subject will last well into old age. A thoroughly good Line of Health will counteract the evil effects of a poor Line of Life, being an indication of good digestion, which will always prove a powerful agent in prolonging life.

526.
Base of the line.

The line should not be joined to that of the life at its base, but just separated, as at *d* in Plate XVII.—this will indicate long life ; joined at this point with the Line of Life, it is a sure indication of weakness of the heart.

527.
Absent.

This line completely absent from a hand is an excellent sign, and will render the subject vivacious in conversation, agile and quick in manner.

528.
Evil conditions of the line.
Color.

If the line is thick and blunt, it is a sign of sickness in old age ; if it is very straight and thin, it is a sign of rigidity of spirit and manner. Red at the upper end, it betrays a tendency to headaches ; thin and red in the centre, it is a sign of fever ; red at the lower end is a sign of a weak heart; thus it will be seen that any unevenness of color in this line is bad. Very red throughout its length indicates brutality and pride. A twisted and wavy liver line is a sign of biliousness, and very often of dishonesty, of which it is, at any rate, a strong confirmatory indication. Much broken or cut into, the line will betray a weak digestion.

Forked at the top so as to make a triangle with the Line of Head [as at *c* in Plate XVII.], it gives a great love of honors and power, combined *always* with a marvellous aptitude and capacity for occult sciences.

529.
Forked at top.

A *coming* sickness marks itself on this line by a little, deep cross-line; a past sickness marks only the life or head lines, leaving merely a gap in the Line of Health.

530.
Sicknesses.

The Line of Health making a good clear triangle with the Lines of Head and of Fortune, we find a subject very clever at natural magic, electro-biology, and the like, a great student of nature and of natural phenomena, with a high faculty of intuition, sometimes accompanied by second-sight.

531.
Clear triangle.

The line traced across the Mount of the Moon is a sure sign of caprice and of change in the course of the life of the subject.

532.
Going to ☽.

A long island at the base of the line denotes a somnambulist.

533.
Island.

A sister line to this liver line indicates strong and unprincipled avarice.

534.
Sister line.

CHAPTER VIII.

The Via Lasciva.

535.
Position.

THIS line is rare; it is often confounded with the Line of Health, and is still more often regarded as a sister line, but it is quite a separate line of itself, appearing only *conjointly with* the Line of Head, though it diverges considerably from it, in the manner shown in the Map of the Hand.

536.
Indications of the line.

It generally betokens cunning, and often faithlessness, especially if twisted, though these indications are considerably modified the

537.
Ascending to the Mount of ☿.

more distinct it be from the Line of Health. It gives ardor and fervor to the passions, and reaching up to the Mount of Mercury, it indicates constant good-luck arising from eloquence and pure talent.

538.
Stars.

Stars on the line generally betoken riches, but often they betray serious troubles and struggles in front of, and accompanying them.

Joined to ☉.

Joined by a ray to the Line of Apollo, the line is a sure indication of wealth.

539.
Joined to ♀.

It used to be customary to look upon this line [as its ancient name denotes] as a sign of lasciviousness, but this indication only belongs to it if it runs across into the Mount of Venus.

CHAPTER IX.

The Girdle of Venus.

THIS line, fortunately not universal, may be taken, as a whole, **540.** General character. to be a *bad* sign in any hand, indicating a tendency to debauchery which it is extremely difficult to conquer.

To a good hand, however, this line will expend itself by giving **541.** In a good hand. energy and ardor in every undertaking entered into by the subject, and this favorable influence of the line is the more certain if it is clear, neat, and going off upon the Mount of Mercury, as at *ll* in Plate XIV. To a good hand this will give merely love of pleasure and energy therein.

It generally makes a subject hysterical and nervous, with a **542.** Effect of the line. great tendency towards spiritualism and sorcery, accompanied by a more or less chronic state of melancholy and depression.

If the Lines of Fortune or of Apollo are cut by the Girdle of **543.** Cutting Fate or ☉. Venus, so as apparently to shatter them in two at this point on the mount, it is a sign of obstacles to success, and misfortunes, probably the result of excessive passion or ardor in the pursuit of pleasure.

Coming up on to the Mount of Mercury, as at *l* in Plate XII., **544.** On to ☿. the subject will add to all the other evil indications of the line the vices of lying and theft.

Cut upon the Mount of Apollo by a short, deep line [as at *o* in **545.** Cut upon ☉. Plate XIII.], it is a sign of loss of fortune, caused by dissipation.

Crossed by a quantity of little lines, it is a sure sign of a **546.** Hysteria. hysterical nature, especially if the Mount of Venus or of the Moon, or both, are highly developed.

547.
Retrospect.

We have now considered the principal lines, and discussed them with considerable minuteness; a careful retrospect will show the reader that the indications of the lines are easily found by examining their condition with reference to the mounts and the other lines of the palm, each mount or line having its peculiar significations and effects, and bringing them to bear upon the *other* mounts and lines and the qualities indicated by them, by juxtaposition or connection with them by means of lines, rays, or signs.

548.
Chance
lines.

Often, however, we find lines in a hand which cannot be accounted for by any of the foregoing rules, and these [which are called "chance lines"] are made the special subject of a future chapter. The signs found in the palm, though they have frequently been adverted to in the previous sub-section, will be our next consideration, with reference to their special and individual significations.

SUB-SECTION V.

(*PLATE IX.*)

THE SIGNS IN THE PALM.

GREAT attention must be paid to the signs which are found very frequently upon, or close to, the mounts and lines of the hands, for they very greatly modify and alter the recognized significations of the mounts or lines, and generally carry with them an indication entirely their own.

549.
Their importance.

CHAPTER I.

The Star.

550.
Indication.
A STAR [Fig. 10, Plate IX.], wherever it appears, is generally the indication of some event we cannot possibly control; it is generally a danger, and always something unavoidable. Whether, however, it is good or bad, depends of course upon the aspect of the lines, particularly of the Line of Fortune. This, however, is fixed—that a star, wherever it is found, always means *something*, and what that something is, be it the task of the cheirosophist to discover.

551.
On ♃.
On the Mount of Jupiter it signifies gratified ambition, good-luck, honor, love, and success. With a cross on this mount it indicates a happy marriage with some one of brilliant antecedents or high position.

552.
On ♄.
On the Mount of Saturn it indicates a great fatality, generally a very bad one, indicating, with corroborative signs, probable murder, and in a criminal or otherwise very bad hand, a probability of death upon the scaffold.

553.
On ☉.
On the Mount of Apollo, with no Line of Apollo in the hand, it betokens wealth without happiness, and celebrity after a hazardous struggle for it. *With* the Line of Brilliancy it denotes excessive celebrity, as the combined result of labor and talent; with several lines also on the mount, it is a sure indication of wealth.

554.
On ☿ or ♂.
On the Mount of Mercury it betrays dishonesty and theft; on the Mount of Mars, violence leading to homicide.

555.
On ☽.
On the Mount of the Moon it indicates hypocrisy and dissimulation, with misfortune resulting from excess of the imagination.

The old cheiromants looked upon this as a warning of death by drowning, and stated that, combined with a high mount invaded by the Line of Head, it indicated suicide by drowning.

On the *base* of the Mount of Venus it indicates a misfortune brought about by the influence of women.

556
On base of ♀.

On the first [or outer] phalanx of any finger [but especially of that of Saturn], a star is a sign of good fortune. On the third [or lowest] phalanx of the finger of Saturn, a star warns the subject of a danger of assassination, and if at this point it is joined by the Line of Saturn, a disgraceful death is almost inevitable, resulting, as a rule, from the vices shown elsewhere in the hand.

557.
On the phalanges of the fingers.
On ♄.

On the base of the phalanx of logic of the thumb—in fact, on the junction of the phalanx of logic and the Mount of Venus—it points to a misfortune connected with a woman, probably indicating an unhappy marriage, which will be the curse of the subject's whole existence, unless the Mount of Jupiter be developed, in which case there is a probability that the subject will get over it.

558.
On the thumb.

A star on a voyage line [668 and 396] indicates with certainty death by drowning.

559.
On a voyage line.

If a star be found in the centre of a quadrangle, the subject, though true and honest as the day, will be the absolute plaything of woman, a trait which will result in a misfortune, from which, however, he will recover in time.

560.
In the quadrangle.

Thus it will be seen that a star is almost the most important sign to seek for in a hand.

561.
Its importance.

10

CHAPTER II.

The Square, the Spot, and the Circle.

562.
Effect.

THE appearance of a square [Fig. 11, Plate IX.] on the hand always denotes power or energy of the qualities indicated by the mount or line on which it is found. It is a sign of good-sense, and of cold, unimpassioned justice.

563.
Appearance and position.

It may either appear as a neat, quadrangular figure, traced as if with a punch, or it may be formed of the [apparently] accidental crossing of principal and chance lines. It will often appear enclosing a bad sign, from the effects of which it entirely protects the subject.

564.
Protection.

Wherever it is found, it always denotes protection; thus round a break in the Line of Life [425 and 497] it betokens recovery from a serious illness; or on the Line of Saturn, it will protect the subject from the evil effects of a badly formed line, or of bad signs found thereon.

565.
With star on ♄.

A star on the Mount of Saturn surrounded by a square denotes an escape from assassination; a square with red points at the corners denotes a preservation from fire.

566.
On ♀.

The square has one evil signification—that is, when it is on the Mount of Venus, close to the Line of Life; under these circumstances it is a warning of imprisonment of some sort or another.

The Spot.

567.
Its indication.

A spot [Fig. 12, Plate IX.], wherever found and of whatever color, always denotes a malady; placed upon a line, it is nearly always the mark of a wound; on the Line of Head it denotes a blow to the head, and consequent folly.

A white spot on the Line of Heart denotes a conquest in love ; a white spot on the Line of Head points to a scientific discovery. A red spot is the sign of a wound ; a black or blue spot is the sign of a disease, generally of a *nervous* character. The white spot is the only comparatively harmless one.

568.
Color.

The Circle.

The circle [Fig 13, Plate IX.] is a comparatively rare sign, which has only one good signification—that is, when it appears on the Mount of Apollo, where it indicates glory and success.

569.
On ☉.

On the Mount of the Moon it denotes danger of death by drowning ; on any other mount it gives a dangerous brilliancy.

570.
On ☽.

On any line it is bad, denoting an injury to the organ or quality represented. Thus, on the Line of Heart it betrays weakness of the heart, and on the Line of Head it forewarns a subject of blindness.

571.
On the lines.

CHAPTER III.

The Island and the Triangle.

572.
Its distinctness.
THE island [Fig. 14, Plate IX.] should perhaps more properly have been noticed in treating of the lines generally; but it is a sign so distinct from any ordinary formation of the line, that it has been though best to consider it in this place as a sign proper.

573.
Its indications.
An island means always one of two things; either it is the mark of something disgraceful, or else it betrays an hereditary evil. It is the more often an hereditary malady of the line, as, for instance, on the Line of Head it will show an hereditary weakness of the head, or on the Line of Heart it betrays an hereditary heart disease, and so on.

574.
Evil indications.
As for the disgraceful indications of the island, it should be taken to mean more properly that the *chance, i.e.,* the temptation, will occur; but a long Line of Head and a strong phalanx of will on the thumb will always annul the most evilly disposed island.

575.
On Line of Heart.
On the Line of Heart it means, in a good hand, heart disease, or, in a bad one, adultery.

576.
On Line of Head.
On the Line of Head, if it occur on the Plain of Mars, it shows a murderous tendency; if *beyond* the Plain of Mars, it betrays evil thoughts. On a good hand it will merely indicate hereditary head weakness.

577.
On liver line.
On the Line of Liver, or Health, it betrays a tendency to theft or dishonesty; in a good hand, a weak digestion, or an an intestinal complaint.

578.
On Life.
On the Line of Life an island indicates some mystery connected with the birth.

The Triangle.

The triangle [Fig. 15, Plate IX.] always denotes aptitude for **579.** science, and may be formed either neatly and by itself, or by the Itsindica-tion. [apparently] chance coincidence of three lines.

On the Mount of Jupiter it indicates diplomatic ability. On the **580.** Mount of Saturn it betrays aptitude for occult sciences and necro- On the mounts. mancy, a sign which becomes very sinister and evil if there be also a star on the third phalanx of this finger. On the Mount of Apollo a triangle indicates science in art ; on the Mount of Mercury, talent in politics ; on the Mount of Mars, science in war ; on the Mount of the Moon, wisdom in mysticism ; and on the Mount of Venus, cal-culation and interest in love.

CHAPTER IV.

The Cross and the "Croix Mystique."

581.
Its effect.

THE cross [Fig. 16, Plate IX.] is seldom a favorable sign, unless it is *very* clearly and well marked, when, by accentuating the qualities of the mount or line, it may have a good signification. It nearly *always* indicates a change of position.

582.
On ♃.

Its one undoubtedly *good* signification is when it appears on the Mount of Jupiter, when it denotes a happy marriage, especially if the Lines of Saturn or of Apollo start from the Mount of the Moon [330].

583.
On ♄.

On the Mount of Saturn it denotes error and fanaticism in religion or occult science, leading to the more evil forms of mysticism.

584.
On ☉.

On the Mount of Apollo it betrays errors of judgment in art, unless there be also a fine Line of Apollo, which will give to the cross the significations of wealth.

585.
On ☿.

On the Mount of Mercury it indicates dishonesty, and even theft.

586.
On ♂.

On the Mount of Mars it denotes danger arising from quarrelsomeness and obstinacy.

587.
On ☽.

A cross on the Mount of the Moon will indicate, if it is large, a man who deceives even himself; but if it is small, it will merely indicate follies of the imagination.

588.
On ♀.

On the Mount of Venus it denotes a single and a fatal love, unless another cross appear on the Mount of Jupiter [330] to render the union happy.

At the bottom of the hand, near the Line of Life—*i.e.*, in the lower angle of the triangle—a cross denotes a struggle, ending in a change of position in life, which is the more radical according as the cross is more or less clearly marked at this point.

589.
At the base
of the hand.

The " Croix Mystique."

This sign is found traced with more or less distinctness in the quadrangle beneath the finger of Saturn.

590.
Its position.

It always gives to a subject mysticism, superstition, and occultism, or, with a very good hand, religion. If it is very large, it betrays exaggerated superstition, bigotry, and hallucination.

591.
Its indica-
tions.

If it is clearly traced in both hands, it betrays folly arising from the excessive influence of the principal mount; thus, with Jupiter developed, over-ambition; with Saturn, misanthropy; with Apollo, extreme vanity or miserliness; and with Venus, erotomania.

592.
In both
hands.

If the "Croix Mystique" is joined to the Line of Saturn, it foretells good fortune arising from religion.

593.
Joined to ♄.

If it is displaced, so as to lie, as it were, between the Mounts of Mars and of the Moon [as at *p* in Plate XIII.], it indicates a changeability of disposition which will lead to good fortune.

594.
Displace-
ment.

CHAPTER V.

The Grille.

595.
Its indications.

THE grille [Fig. 17, Plate IX.] is generally the indication of obstacles, and of the faults of a mount whereon it is found. But if there be no mount particularly elevated in the hand, it will so emphasize a mount, if it is found upon one, as to make *it* the principal mount and keynote of the interpretation of the hand.

596.
On the mounts.
♃.
♄.
☉.

On the Mount of Jupiter it indicates superstition, egoism, pride, and the spirit of domination.

On the Mount of Saturn it foretells misfortune and want of luck.

On the Mount of Apollo it betrays folly and vanity, and a great desire of glory, joined to impotence and error.

☿.

On the Mount of Mercury it tells of a serious tendency towards theft, cunning, and dishonesty.

♂.

On the Mount of Mars it forewarns a violent death, or, at any rate, some great danger thereof.

☽.

A grille on the Mount of the Moon indicates sadness, restlessness, discontent, and a morbid imagination.

597.
On ☽ with a lined hand.

If on a hand which is much covered with lines [316], it shows a constant movement and state of excitement. If there be a star on the Mount of Saturn, this sign tells of the wildest exaltations, nervous spasms, and continual anxieties and disquietude. With a well-traced Line of Apollo and a grille on the Mount of the Moon we find poetry, and great talent for lyrics and literature.

598.
On ♀.

The grille on the Mount of Venus is often a bad sign, denoting lasciviousness and morbid curiosity, especially with the Girdle of

Venus traced in the hand. With a strong phalanx of will, and a long Line of Head, and the Line of Apollo, or Brilliancy, this sign merely results in a nervous excitement, which is in no way pernicious or evil in its effects, giving a refinement and daintiness to the passions.

A strong phalanx of will, with a good Line of Head and of Apollo, will *always* greatly modify the sinister effects of the grille, *excepting* when it is found on the Mounts of Jupiter or Saturn, when it is practically irremediable.

599.
Modifying
signs.

CHAPTER VI.

The Signs of the Planets.

600.
Effects.

BESIDES the above comparatively ordinary signs, we find in some instances [though such instances are *excessively* rare] the actual sign of a planet actually traced on a mount. As a rule, when this occurs the rest of the hand is perfectly plain, the whole force of the character being concentrated in the quality indicated by the " precipitation " of the planetary sign.

601.
Combinations.

The sign of Mercury [☿] traced upon the Mount of Jupiter gives great administrative talent and noble eloquence. The sign of the Moon [☽] on the Mount of Jupiter leads to intense mysticism and error. The sign of Mercury on the Mount of Apollo gives great celebrity and eloquence in science.

602.
On its own mount.

A mount sometimes also, instead of being high or rayed, has its own sign traced upon it; thus ♃ on Jupiter, ♄ on Saturn, ☉ on Apollo, ☿ on Mercury, ♂ on Mars, ☽ on the Moon, and ♀ on Venus. These signs, of course, intensify the qualities of the mounts to an extremely marked and extraordinary extent.

SUB-SECTION VI.

THE SIGNS UPON THE FINGERS.

IN the preceding sub-section we have dealt only with the signs found upon the palm of the hand. We have also to consider the lines and signs which find themselves traced upon the fingers, which signs have also their special significations.

603. Lines on the first phalanx.

Lines on the first phalanx of a finger always denote a weakness or failing of the quality of the finger. If the lines are twisted and confused, they foreshadow danger to the subject from the qualities of the finger. A single deep ray on the first phalanx of a finger indicates an idealism or folly connected with the quality.

604. Lines connecting the phalanges.

Lines from the first into the second phalanges unite, as it were, the worlds of idealism and reason [41], causing the subject to mix a certain amount of reason with all the promptings of his imagination. In the same way, lines connecting the second and third phalanges unite reason and matter, and the subject will always set about his worldly affairs in a reasonable and sensible manner.

One short line, sharply traced on each phalanx of each finger, is a prognostic of sudden death.

605. One line on each phalanx.

Lines running the entire length of the fingers give energy and ardor to the qualities of the finger ; cross lines, however, are obstacles in the way of the proper development of the characteristics of the finger.

606. Lines all along the fingers.

CHAPTER I.

Signs on the First, or Index Finger.

607.
Line to
second pha-
lanx.

A LINE extending from the mount, through the third phalanx into the second, gives a character in which reason and thought are mingled with audacity.

608.
Cross lines.

Cross lines on the third phalanx indicate inheritances, according to the older cheirosophists; on the second phalanx they denote envy and falsehood. Lines across the tips of the fingers denote general debility; and if they extend all the way from one side of the nail round the ball of the finger to the other side, they foreshadow wounds to the head.

609.
Crosses.

A pair of crosses on the second phalanx is a sign of the friendship of great men.

610.
Stars.

A star on the first phalanx indicates great good fortune; a star on the second phalanx indicates mischief and boldness, unless it is connected with the first phalanx by a line, in which case it becomes a sign of modesty. A star on the third phalanx is a sign of unchastity.

611.
Crescent.

A crescent upon the first phalanx is a sure sign of imprudence, which may bring about very grave results.

CHAPTER II.

Signs on the Second, or Middle Finger.

A LINE from the Mount of Saturn across the third phalanx of the finger indicates prosperity in arms; if it is oblique, it foretells death in battle. **612.** Into third phalanx.

Many lines just penetrating into the mount denote cruelty; if they go the whole length of the finger they indicate melancholy; or, if they are very parallel and equal, they denote success in mining operations. If the lines are confined to the first phalanx, they denote avarice. Twisted lines on the third phalanx denote ill-luck. **613.** Lines.

A triangle on the third phalanx indicates mischief and ill-luck. **614.** Triangle.

A cross in the same place indicates sterility in a female hand. **615.** Cross.

A star on the first phalanx indicates great misfortune, and if it is on the *side* of the finger it betrays a probability of death, which will, however, be in a just cause. **616.** Star.

CHAPTER III.

Signs on the Third, or Ring Finger.

617.
Lines.

A SINGLE line running the entire length of the finger is a sure indication of great renown. Many lines are a sign of losses, probably occasioned by women.

618.
Lines on the third phalanx.

Straight lines on the third phalanx indicate prudence and happiness. Turning to one side of the finger they indicate great success, but not success accompanied by wealth. If the lines on the third phalanx penetrate on to the mount they indicate good fortune, accompanied by loquacity and often by arrogance.

619.
From third into second.

A line extending from the third phalanx into the second is a sign of goodness and cleverness, accompanied by good fortune. Cross lines placed upon this phalanx indicate difficulties in the way which will have to be surmounted.

620.
Crescent.

A crescent on the third phalanx signifies unhappiness, and a cross at the same place signifies extravagance.

CHAPTER IV.

Signs on the Fourth, or Little Finger.

A LINE throughout the length of this finger is a signification of success in science, and uprightness of mind; three lines similarly running right down the finger are a sign of research in chimerical and impossible sciences.

621.
Lines.

Deep lines on the first phalanx denote weakness of constitution; a cross on the same place is significant of poverty and *consequent* celibacy.

622.
On the first phalanx.

Lines on the second phalanx are an indication of research in occult sciences. If they are confused and coarse, they betray unchastity.

623.
On the second phalanx.

A line from the third into the second phalanx indicates eloquence and consequent success. If the line is twisted, it gives great sharpness and cunning in defence of self. If this line start from the mount, it is a still surer sign of prosperity and success.

624.
From third to second phalanx.

One thick line, or a cross on a third phalanx, betrays a tendency to theft. A star on the same phalanx denotes eloquence.

625.
A cross, or star.

A line extending from the mount into the third phalanx is significant of great intelligence and astuteness.

626.
Line to third phalanx.

CHAPTER V.

Signs on the Thumb.

SIGNS are much rarer upon the thumb than upon fingers, but still they are sometimes found.

627.
Several lines.

A subject who has several lines on the phalanx of will traced along the entire length, will make a faithful lover, having the gift of constancy and fidelity.

628.
Cross lines.

Cross lines upon the thumb denote riches.

629.
From ♀ to logic.

Lines extending from the mount on to the phalanx of logic, are a sure sign that the subject is much beloved.

630.
Star on logic.

A star on the phalanx of logic in a female hand is a sign of great riches.

631.
Ring round the joint.

A ring right around the joint which separates the phalanges of will and logic was held by the older cheiromants to be the sign of the scaffold.

SUB-SECTION VII.

THE TRIANGLE, THE QUADRANGLE, AND THE RASCETTE.

CHAPTER I.

The Triangle.

THE triangle [called also the Triangle of Mars, from the fact that it is filled by the Plain of Mars] is the name given to the triangular space enclosed between the Lines of Life, Head, and Health. When [as is often the case, 524] the Line of Health is not present in a hand, or so very badly traced as to be almost invisible, its place must be supplied by an imaginary line drawn from the base of the Line of Life to the end of the Line of Head, *or*, this side of the triangle may be formed of the Line of Apollo.

632. Its position and construction.

Though it must be considered as a whole, still each part of the triangle has its special signification; thus, it is composed of the UPPER ANGLE formed by the junction of the Lines of Life and Head; the INNER ANGLE, formed by the junction of the Lines of Head and Health; and the LOWER ANGLE, formed by the junction of the Lines of Health and Life. [The lower angle may also be formed of the junction of the Lines of Health and of Fortune.]

633. Its composition.

If the triangle is well traced and neat, being composed of good, even lines [as in Plate XVII.], it indicates good health, good-luck, a long life, and a courageous disposition.

634. Neat and clean.

If it is large, it denotes audacity, liberality of mind, generosity, and nobleness of soul; to have these significations it must be well and healthfully colored, not livid, nor approaching to deep red.

635. Large and well colored.

11

636.
Small and curved.
If it is small and formed of lines curving much inwards, it betrays pettiness, cowardice, and avarice.

637.
Its growth.
Sometimes a triangle will form itself in a hand which began by being absolutely without it ; this is a sign that the health, originally bad, has improved with advancing years.

638.
Rough skin.
If the skin inside the triangle is rough and hard, it is an indication of hardihood and strength of nerve.

639.
Cross in the centre.
A cross in the triangle denotes an extremely quarrelsome and contrary disposition. Many crosses in the triangle betoken continual bad-luck.

640.
Crescents.
A crescent in the triangle, as at *f* in Plate XVII., betrays an extremely capricious disposition, often indicating brutality and a love of bullying. If it is joined to the Line of Head, as at *g* in the same figure, it is a prognostic of a violent death brought upon one's self by an imprudence or a want of calculation. Joined, however, similarly to the Line of Health, as at *h*, it is a sign of power and of success accompanied by excellent health.

641.
Star.
A star in the triangle denotes riches, but riches obtained with much difficulty and worry. If the star is the termination of a worry line it indicates a sorrow, and if. the worry line come from a star in the Mount of Venus, it denotes that the sorrow has resulted from the death of a parent or of some near relation.

The Upper Angle.

642.
Proper formation.
The upper angle [*i*, in Plate XVII.] should be neat, clearly traced, and well pointed ; it indicates refinement and delicacy of mind.

643.
Bluntness.
Blunt and short, it betrays a heavy, dull intellect, and a want of delicacy. *Very* blunt—*i.e.*, placed under the Mount of Saturn—it betrays a great danger of misery, and a tendency to avarice.

644.
Very pointed.
The other extreme, however—*i.e.*, *very* pointed—is a sign of malignity, envy, and finesse.

The Inner Angle.

The inner angle [*k*, in Plate XVII.], if clear and well marked, indicates long life and a quick intelligence.

Very sharp, it betrays a highly nervous temperament, and nearly always a mischievous disposition.

Obtuse and confused, this angle denotes heaviness of intelligence, dulness of instinct, and, as a resulting consequence, obstinacy and inconstancy.

The Lower Angle.

The lower angle [*l*, in Plate XVII.], well defined, and just open [as at *d*], gives strong indications of good health and a good heart. If it is too sharp—in fact, if it is closed up—it denotes avarice and debility.

If it is heavy and coarse, composed of many rays, or of a confusion of lines, it betrays a bad nature, with a strong tendency to rudeness and laziness.

Thus it will be seen that it is most important to observe, with reference to its component lines, the formation of the triangle and of its constituent angles.

The Quadrangle.

The quadrangle [see Map, Plate VII.] is the square space contained between the Lines of Heart and of Head. It may be said to be bounded at its two ends by imaginary lines, drawn perpendicularly to the Line of Head from the crevice between the first and second fingers, and from the crevice between the third and fourth fingers.

651.
Proper aspect.
It should be fairly large and wide at the two ends [but not too narrow in the centre], clearly distinguishable, and of a smooth surface comparatively free from lines; under these aspects it indicates fidelity, loyalty, and an equable disposition.

652.
Narrow in centre.
Too narrow in the centre, it betrays malignity, injustice, and deceit, often accompanied by avarice. If it is much wider under the Mount of Mercury than under that of Saturn, it betrays a degeneration from generosity to avarice. Narrow under the Mount of Mercury, it denotes a more or less continual anxiety about reputation.

653.
Too wide.
Too large and wide throughout its extent, it signifies imprudence, or even folly, and this is so even when there are other signs denoting prudence in the hand.

654.
Much lined.
The quadrangle much filled up with little lines is a sign of a weak head.

655.
Badly traced.
If it is so badly traced as to be almost invisible as to its boundaries, it is a signification of misfortune, and of a malignant, mischievous character.

656.
" Croix Mystique."
It must be remembered [590] that it is in the quadrangle that we search for the " Croix Mystique."

657.
Star.
A well-colored and well-formed star is a great indication of truth and trustworthiness. Such a subject is pliable, and can easily be dealt with by fair means [especially by women]; such subjects generally make very considerable fortunes by their own merit.

658.
Line to ☿.
A line from the quadrangle to the Mount of Mercury betokens the patronage and protection of the great.

CHAPTER II.

The Rascette, or the Three Bracelets.

THESE are the names given to the wrist and Bracelets of Life [see Map, Plate VII.], the entire region being known as the rascette, and the lines traced across it as the Bracelets of Life.

The Bracelets of Life are so called because each is said to be the indication of twenty-five to thirty years of life. A long practice has proved that in ninety-nine cases out of every hundred a Bracelet of Life gives about twenty-five to twenty-seven years of life, and even when the Line of Life is short a well-braceleted rascette will still insure a long life to the subject.

Three lines clearly and neatly traced denote health, wealth, good-luck, and a tranquil life. The clearer the lines the better is the general health of the subject.

If the first line is chained, we find a laborious life, but good fortune resulting therefrom.

If the lines are altogether badly formed, it is a sign of extravagance.

A cross in the centre of the rascette, as at *m* in Plate XII., is a sign of a hard life, ending with good fortune and quietude.

An angle in the rascette, as at *m* in Plate XV., is a sign of inheritances and of honors in old age. To this will be added good health if a cross appear in this angle, as at *i* in Plate XVI.

If the Bracelets of Life break into points converging towards the base of the Line of Saturn, it is a sign of lying and vanity.

659. The rascette; its composition.

660. "Bracelets of Life."

661. Three clear lines.

662. Chained.

663. Badly formed.

664. Cross.

665. Angle and cross.

666. Pointing upwards.

667.
Star.

A star in the centre of the rascette will mean inheritances in a lucky hand, but unchastity in a weak, sensual hand.

668.
Voyage
lines.

Lines from the rascette extending upon the Mount of the Moon signify voyages. A line right up to the Mount of Jupiter will signify a very long voyage indeed; in fact, the distance of the voyages may be told from the length of the lines. If the lines converge towards the Mount of Saturn, but do not join there, it is an indication that the subject will not return from the voyage. One of them, ending on the Line of Life, denotes probability of death upon the voyage. If the lines are absolutely parallel throughout their course, the voyages will be profitable, but dangerous.

669.
Line to ☿

A line from the rascette straight up to the Mount of Mercury is a prognostic of sudden and unexpected wealth.

670.
Line to ☉.

A similar line going to the Mount of Apollo is a mark of the favor and protection of some great person.

671.
Line to
Health
through ☽.

A line from the rascette near the percussion of the hand, passing through the Mount of the Moon to join the Line of the Liver or Health, is a sign of sorrow and adversity, especially if the line be unequal and poorly traced.

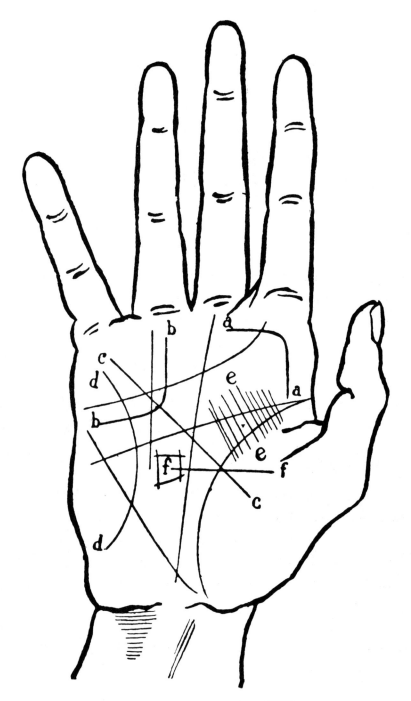

PLATE XVIII.—CHANCE LINES.

SUB-SECTION VIII.

CHANCE LINES.

WE have now arrived at a point from which, having carefully
discussed all the regular details of cheirosophy, it is necessary
that we should turn to the consideration of certain lines which
appear from time to time in the hand, and which, having special
significations of their own, cannot be taken account of whilst going
categorically through the indications of the principal lines, and of
the various combinations of them. Their number is, of course,
practically unlimited, for they form themselves according, to the
characters and lives of individual subjects. The student will find
after a time that, as the groundwork of cheiromancy impresses itself
upon him, he will be able at once to read the indications of any line
which may be shown to him, though he may never have seen one
like it before. The following instances, therefore, are not given as
being in any way a complete list of the "chance lines," but are
subjoined as a kind of guide for the student, to enable him to
decipher these "eclectic indications" whensoever and wheresoever
he may find them. The following instances are, for the most part,
illustrated in Plates XVIII., XIX., and XX., so that there will be
no difficulty in remembering their exact positions. In these figures
the principal lines are *drawn*, but only the chance lines are lettered
and referred to.

A line starting from the commencement of the Line of Life, going
to the Mount of Jupiter, and then turning on to the Mount of

672.
Definition of
chance lines.

673.
From Life
to ♃ and ♄.

Saturn, as at *aa* in Plate XVIII., denotes a disposition to fashionable fanaticism. If such a subject is religious *at all*, it will be that he is actuated mainly by a desire to become eminent in that particular line.

674.
From ♂ under Heart to ☉.
A line starting from the Mount of Mars, running under the Line of Heart, and turning up to the Mount of Apollo, as at *bb* in Plate XVIII., indicates a determination to attain celebrity so deeply rooted that the subject whose hand bears this line will attain that celebrity by *any* means.

675.
From ♀ to ☿.
A line barring the whole hand from the Mount of Venus to that of Mercury denotes cleverness and intelligence, arising from an affair of the heart, or from the promptings of passion.

676.
Worry lines.
We have in another place discussed worry lines [428], which are, after all, a species of chance line; any worry line which starts from a star on the Mount of Venus denotes that some one very dearly beloved has died.

677.
From ♀ to ♂.
Star.
Two worry lines, extending parallel from the Mount of Venus to that of Mars, denote the pursuit of two love affairs at the same time, and a star joined to these lines denotes that the pursuit has ended in disaster.

678.
Curved from ☿ to ☽.
A curved line, extending from the Mount of Mercury to that of the Moon [as at *dd* in Plate XVIII.] is a signification of presentiments and occult powers. Such a subject, if his Line of Head decline upon the Mount of the Moon, will have great powers as a medium.

679.
Chained Heart and line from ♀ to ☿.
Point.
If, with a chained Line of Heart, a line from the Mount of Venus touch it underneath the Mount of Mercury [as at *aa* in Plate XIX.], it is a sign that the whole life has been disturbed and worried by a woman [or *vice versâ* in a female hand]. A black point on this line [as at *b* in Plate XIX.] signifies widowhood or widowerhood.

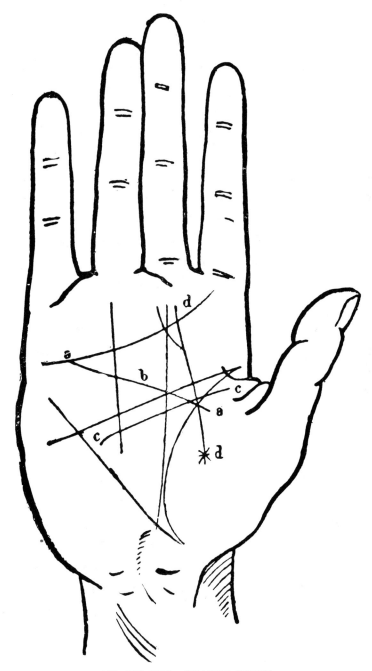

PLATE XIX.—CHANCE LINES.

A line from the Mount of Venus cutting the Line of Apollo [as at *cc* in Plate XIX.] denotes a misfortune at the time indicated by the point at which the line cuts through the Line of Life. If it cut through in early life, the misfortune was connected with the parents of the subject.

680. From ♀ to Line of ☉.

Quantities of little rays across the Line of Life into the quadrangle [as at *ee* in Plate XVIII.], accompanied by short nails, are a certain sign of quantities of little worries, estrangements of friends, etc., occasioned by the spirit of argument and criticism, and the love of teasing which the subject has, as indicated by the short nails.

681. Rays across the Line of Life.

A line extending from a star on the Mount of Venus to a fork under the finger of Saturn [as at *dd* in Plate XIX.] betrays an unhappy marriage.

682. From ♀ to ♄.

A line starting from the Mount of Venus, and ending in a square in the palm of the hand [any part], as at *ff* in Plate XVIII., is significant of a narrow escape from marriage with a scoundrel, or with an extremely wicked woman.

683. From ♀ into palm.

A long island, extending from the Mount of Venus to that of Saturn, with a similar island in the Line of Fortune, both at the points representing the same age [Plate XI.], as at *a* and *b* in Plate XX., indicates seduction.

684. Island from ♀ to ♄.

A line going from a star on the Mount of Venus to the Plain of Mars, and then turning up to the Mount of Apollo, where it meets a single ray [as at *cc* in Plate XX.], foretells a great inheritance from the death of a near relation.

685. From ♀ to ♂ and ☉.

A *quantity* of little lines on the percussion, at the side of the Mount of Mercury [as at *d* in Plate XX.], indicate levity and inconstancy [364], especially if the Mounts of Venus and of the Moon are highly developed.

686. Many little lines on the percussion.

687.
Method of
interpreta-
tion.

These few instances will be sufficient to explain the method of interpreting chance lines. It will be observed that they are read carefully with reference to the mounts and lines which they cross throughout their course, and according to the signs which meet and interrupt them.

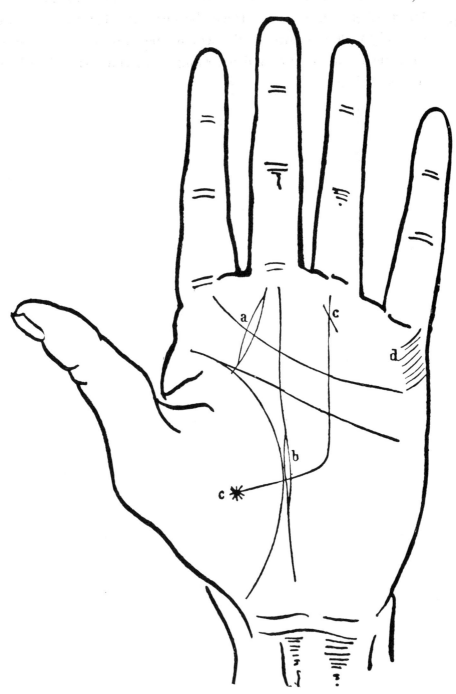

PLATE XX.—CHANCE LINES.

SUB-SECTION IX.

A FEW ILLUSTRATIVE TYPES.

In this section are described a few types of character and of profession ; that is to say, the collected signs and formations which indicate certain conditions of mind, with the probable effects of those conditions upon the subject, as regards his choice of a profession or his walk in life.

688.
Collective
indications.

For instance, take a hand which betrays a murderous or homicidal tendency ; in this hand you will find the general complexion to be very red, or very livid ; if the former, the tendency to murder arises from fury and momentary fits of anger ; if the latter, the whole instinct of the subject is evil. The first phalanx of the finger of Mercury will be heavily lined, and at the base of the Line of Life will [probably] be found a sister line. The Line of Head will be deeply traced and thick, having probably a circle upon it, and being generally joined to the Line of Heart, and separate from the Line of Life, the nails short, the Line of Life thick at the commencement, and spotted with red, and the Line of Head twisted across the hand. All these signs collected in a hand are an infallible indication of a murderous instinct.

689.
Homicide.

Take another example : in this hand we find the Line of Head twisted and very red, a grille is placed upon the Mount of Mercury, and the whole hand is dry and thin, having the joints developed on the fingers. From the third phalanx of the little finger sundry small lines go on to the mount, which latter is also scarred with a

690.
Theft.

deep, strong ray. This is the hand of a thief, and the impulse of theft will be found to be almost [if not quite] insurmountable.

691.
Falsehood.

Falsehood—*i.e.*, a general tendency to deceit—is always very clearly marked in the hand, and is marked by a number of different signs, any one of which by itself is a sufficient indication of a strong tendency in that direction. These are: a high Mount of the Moon, upon which the Line of Head is forked, and on which are found small red points; the thumb is short, and on the inner surfaces of the phalanges of the fingers there appears a kind of hollowing out or sinking in of the flesh. The Line of Head is generally separated from that of life by a space which is filled with a number of confused lines.

692.
Application of Cheirology.

In conversing with a subject in whose hands you have seen all, or any, of these signs, bear in mind what has been said under the heading of Cheirology [SS. I., Chapter XI.].

693.
Sensuality.

Another very characteristic hand is the voluptuous, or pleasure-loving hand. The fingers are smooth and pointed, having the third or lower phalanges swollen; the whole hand is plump and white, the palm strong, and the thumb short, giving it sensitiveness. The Mount of Venus is high. Such subjects are impressionable, and liable to fall into grave errors; they are sensual, vain, and egoists, always actuated by motives of pleasure. Women who have these hands are always dangerous, for they are subtle and unscrupulous in their pursuit of enjoyment, and often exercise a most fatal influence upon men into whose lives they come.

694.
The professions according to Desbarrolles.

Adrien Desbarrolles, in his later and larger work on the science, devotes a considerable space to the indications of various professions. It would be beyond the scope of a work like the present one to go into the matter as fully as he does, but a short *résumé* of his leading principles may not be out of place in a chapter on illustrative types.

Of an artist, the sign is, of course, primarily the artistic hand, but our author goes further. He discusses the various modifications which betoken different classes of painting; thus the flower painter will have the Mount of Venus high, with long fingers and a large thumb [color, detail, and perseverance]; the painter of still life will have rather squared fingers and the Mount of Mercury [exactitude and science]; the painter of battle pieces will have the Mount of Mars developed, indicating the natural taste of the subject. He points out the fact that painters with squared fingers always paint what they can actually see rather than what they merely imagine.

695. Artist's hand.

In a doctor's hand we shall find the Mount of Mercury rayed, with the Line of Apollo clearly traced. The doctor whose hands bear the Mount of the Moon well developed will always be inclined to discoveries and eclecticism, and the doctor with hard hands and very much spatulated fingers will have a natural *penchant* for veterinary surgery.

696. Doctor's hand.

The astronomer has the Mounts of the Moon, of Mercury, and of Saturn well developed, with long, knotty fingers to add calculation to his imagination and his science.

697. Astronomy.

The horticulturist has a hand in which we find the Mounts of Venus and of the Moon high, with spatulate fingers to give him energy, and long fingers to give him detail.

698. Horticulture.

Square fingers, with a good Line of Apollo and a good Line of Jupiter, denote an architect.

699. Architecture.

Sculpture betrays itself by a scarcity of lines, the Mounts of Venus, of Mars, and of the Moon high in the hand, which has a strong tendency to thickness and hardness.

700. Sculpture.

Literary men have always the Mounts of Jupiter and of the Moon developed; the latter particularly, if the taste lies in the direction of poetry. Literature gives, as a rule, soft spatulate or square

701. Literature.

hands, with the joints [especially that of matter (the second)] slightly developed. Literary critics have always short nails and high Mounts of Mercury.

702.
Music.

Among musicians [198] execution is the domain of subjects whose fingers are spatulate and whose Mount of Saturn is high, whose nails are short and whose joints are developed, with the Mount of the Moon prominent, long thumbs, the Line of Apollo, and [as a rule] the Girdle of Venus. Melody generally gives smooth fingers with mixed tips, the prevailing mount being that of Venus.

703.
Drama.

The actor has fingers which are either spatulate or square, the Mount of Venus developed, and the Line of Head forked. The Line of Heart turns up slightly towards the Mount of Mercury, and, as a rule, a line runs from the Mount of Mars to that of Apollo.

The above illustrative types from those given by M. Desbarrolles have, by repeated and careful examination, been found to be, with extremely few exceptions, completely correct. Their explanations are easily found [3], and the student will, in a very short time, be able, immediately on seeing a hand, to tell the subject what is his profession.

SUB-SECTION X.

MODUS OPERANDI.

MUCH has been said in works on cheiromancy on the condition of the subject at the time of the examination, his mental and physical state, and so on, but I think that all these things are, to a very great extent, immaterial. The only things to be borne in mind are that the hands should not be too hot nor too cold, and that they should not have just been pulled out of a tight glove, and, above all things, that there should be a good light. The hand should be held in an oblique position as regards the light, so as to throw the lines and formations into relief. With this object in view, also, the fingers should be slightly bent, so as to contract the palm and accentuate the lines, for it must be observed that the hands fold upon the lines, though the lines are not formed by the folding. If it is quite convenient, the morning is the best time to examine a hand, but it is practically immaterial if the cheirosophist has had any experience.

704.
Condition of the hands.

Lastly, in reading a hand, to whomsoever it belongs, you must never hesitate to take it in your own hands and hold it firmly. These short preliminaries being attended to, you will commence your examination. It is far better to examine the whole hand carefully and silently till its indications are quite clear in your own mind, and then to speak promptly and boldly, than to decipher the indications slowly, one after another, reading one tentatively with a view to ascertaining its correctness, before going on to another.

705.
Mode of procedure.

706.
Simplicity
of the
science.

The great thing that I desire to impress upon the minds of my readers is the simplicity of the science. Adrien Desbarrolles, in his advanced work on the science, says: "That which prevents beginners from succeeding immediately in cheiromancy is that they find it too simple, and think it necessary to go beyond it to arrive at something more pretentious, more confused, more difficult, and more impossible to understand. They do not *want* an easily understood science. For many people, a science which is simple is not a science at all; they strive and strive, racking their brains in search of a truth which is at their very hands, and which they can find nowhere else."

707.
Order of the
examination.
Cheirog-
nomy.

Having taken a hand in yours, first you must examine the Line of Life, to see what effects health and the great events of life have had upon the condition of the subject. Next look at the phalanx of will, and see how far it is controlled or influenced by the phalanx of logic. Then you will note the tips of the fingers, seeing also whether they are smooth or whether they have the joints developed, and whether any particular phalanx or set of phalanges is or are longer or more fully developed than the others; this will tell you whether the subject is governed by intuition, by reason, or by material instinct. Then notice whether the fingers are long or short. At first you can hardly tell whether they are long or short, but after a little time you will be able to judge at once of length or shortness by comparison with the other hands you have seen; the same remarks apply to the thumb.

708.
Order of ex-
amination.
Cheiro-
mancy.

You have already noticed whether the hands are soft or hard; now you will turn your attention to the palm, to see what mount or mounts govern the instincts, and how those mounts are governed in turn by primary or secondary lines. Then go back to the Line of Life, and examine the Line of Fortune, noting whether the latter is broken, and if so, search on the mounts for signs to teach you the cause and interpretation of the break. Then examine carefully the Lines of Head and Heart, and the secondary lines, with the signs which may modify their indications. Be careful not to predict a future event from a sign which is evidently that of a past one: a sign which, though visible, is effaced, or quasi-effaced, is that of a past event; a sign which is clear and *well colored* is that of a present circumstance; and a sign which is only just visible, as it were, beneath the surface of the skin, is that of a future event.

Past, present, and future.

709.
Uncommon signs.

Whenever you see a star, a cross, or any other sign in an apparently inexplicable position, you must search the principal lines and the mounts for an explanation. The explanation will often be found in a mark on the Line of Fortune or in a worry line [428]. At the same time look at the Mount of Jupiter, for this will often, by being good, counteract the evil indications of a sign, and at the Mount of Mars, to see whether the subject has that resignation which will give him calm, and even happiness, through whatever circumstances may assail his life.

710.
Exposition of the indications.

When you have examined everything, strike a balance, as it were, noting what signs are contradicted or counteracted by others, and what is, in fact, the whole indication of the hand. Speak boldly, and never mind offending people by what you tell them; what you tell them is *the truth*, and they need not have let you know it. Always warn people that what you shall tell them will be the actual truth, and not a string of complimentary platitudes; and it is also well to ask people not to show you their hands if they have anything to conceal. If, after this, they still persist in having their hands read, say boldly whatever you see there, without caring about the feelings of the subject.

711.
How to take an impression of the hand.

To take an impression of the hand for readings by mail: Smoke a sheet of white paper over lighted lamp without chimney—when black, press right hand firmly on smoked side to insure impression of the palm—wet back of paper with alcohol to set the carbon.

12

Index of Leading Indications.

INDEX OF LEADING INDICATIONS.

The numbers refer to the paragraphs.